master chefs

master chefs

SIMPLY IRRESISTIBLE RECIPES

HarperCollins*Illustrated*

city rhodes city rhodes city rhodes city rhodes
city rhode

foreword

A number of significant changes have taken place since we published our last book, *Simply the Best*. Not least the change in name of our company to Sodexho. This reflects our global presence and the provision of many other services other than catering. The one thing that has not changed is our absolute obsession with the preparation and presentation of great food. The Master Class series, which commenced in late 1994, is a continued commitment to our people working with world-class chefs – developing, learning and acquiring new skills. This is evidenced in this book, with a section where our chefs have devised recipes after being inspired by the Master Chefs. Our working partnership with Gary Rhodes gives us four commercial restaurants – two of which have achieved Michelin stars. Gary's unique and highly innovative food has helped inspire many of our chefs who pass through his kitchens. By the time this book is published we will have completed 36 Master Classes in a variety of our clients' facilities the length and breadth of the country. We bring to you by popular demand 17 menus from these spectacular events.

If you enjoy creative food and great flavours I'm sure you will enjoy this book.

Bon appétit.

David Ford

DAVID FORD
Chief Executive
Sodexho

introduction

I am delighted to bring together a second set of wonderful menus and recipes created by the most talented chefs today (the Masters), who not only are highly innovative in their development of recipes but happen also to be first-class teachers. This rare combination has meant a truly memorable number of Master Classes in which our chefs get the opportunity to work with their culinary heroes. The sub-title of the book came from one of our guests who was working very hard at maintaining their diet but confessed at the end of the evening that the food was 'simply irresistible' – a view echoed by many.

In the last 6 years over 600 chefs have attended the Master Class programme. This programme is simple in its design: we invite 16 of our local chefs to work for the day with the selected Master Chef. He/She instructs them in the dishes which make up the menu and then supervises its production for 100 invited guests, who benefit from the fruits of the local chefs' training. The venues chosen for the programme are locations where we are privileged to work with our clients.

We celebrated our fifth-anniversary Master Class at Lords, broke with tradition and invited 500 guests. Forty of our chefs worked on this large banquet and a number of our previous Master Chefs joined us as guests on the evening. We dedicated the event to our chosen charity, Debra, and this spectacular evening raised, with the help of our Master Chefs, £35,000 for the charity.

We again have a charity link to this book, with Hospitality Action, and our generous Master Chefs have agreed to help once more this year. Sales of *Simply the Best* raised over £7,000 for this industry charity. This year our target is £10,000.

Our first vote of thanks must go to the great chefs who have made this book possible. For his assistance with the descriptions of the wines, I am grateful to Simon Haywood from Matthew Clarke. I would also like to thank the members of the Sodexho team who have worked with me to bring this book to publication. For all his dedicated effort to Master Class and the book – John Whybrew; for their invaluable assistance in food/recipe verifying – Peter Joyner, Paul Eastmead, Paul Burton, Julia Newton and Debbie Kelly-Greaves; for administration excellence – Claire Day and Vicci Field, and for design assistance – Amanda Snow.

I would also like to thank the team at HarperCollins for their patience and professionalism, as well as for being fun to work with.

All the recipes serve 4 people unless otherwise indicated. Enjoy the contents of the book – I did!

Peter Hazzard

PETER HAZZARD
Executive Director – Food Services
Sodexho

CONTENTS

All recipes serve 4 people unless otherwise indicated on the recipe

Introduction 6

paul heathcote 10

menu one 12

artichoke & foie gras soup

seared salmon & poached egg with watercress dressing

fillet of beef with thyme, red wine & root vegetables

rhubarb & elderflower omelette soufflé

paul heathcote

menu two 20

potted salmon with potato salad, soured cream & chive oil

steamed guinea fowl with mash, artichokes, asparagus & yellow wine sauce

raspberry & pistachio brûlée with raspberry sorbet

franco taruschio 28

panzerotti fritti (deep-fried mozzarella pastries)

vincisgrassi (an 18th-century pasta dish – pasta and béchamel sauce enriched with Parma ham, porcini mushrooms and truffle)

crocchette d'eglesino affumicato con salsa d'aragosta (smoked haddock fish cakes with lobster bisque sauce)

quaglie arrosto con salvia e frittedda (roast quail with sage & braised spring vegetables)

trio of coffee desserts:

panna cotta al caffè (coffee-flavoured mascarpone cream)

crema bruciata di caffè (coffee crème brûlée)

gelato al caffè con salsa di caffè (coffee ice cream with coffee sauce)

ross burden 42

salad of kangaroo fillet with crispy shallots

thai fishcakes with dipping sauce

steamed halibut steaks with garlic oil

pad thai

coconut tart with raspberry sauce, star anise ice cream & maraschino sabayon

antony worrall thompson 56

"tapas-style" starter:

shrimp & green onion pancakes

chilli-garlic prawns

vegetable griddle cakes with soured cream & chives

tunisian carrot rolls with apricot dip

skate & sweet spinach salad

truffled burrata with roasted cherry tomatoes

balsamic foie gras

monkfish & mussels in spices

prosciutto-wrapped chicken breast on cep lentils

pavlova roulade with roasted pear

ken hom 72

menu one 74

crispy chicken with ginger sauce crispy wontons

steamed fish with coconut

prawns with green curry

thai barbecue chicken with green bean salad & turmeric rice

thai-style steamed pumpkin custard

ken
hom

menu two 88

thai meatballs

vietnamese-style spring rolls

classic wonton soup

singapore curry crab

thai chicken with hong kong-style broccoli & baby corn

chocolate cake with candied ginger

gary
rhodes 100

ballotine of salmon on caramelised shallots, capers & black olives with a saffron water dressing

roasted tournedos of lamb on seared artichoke filled with a cèpe duxelle

iced vanilla parfait with roasted nutmeg apples

alastair
little 112

filo-wrapped asparagus & prosciutto

tiger prawn chermoula sauté

spinach & ricotta risotto

chicken breast stuffed with porcini mushrooms

apple, prune & zabaglione tart

tony
tobin 126

lasagne of marinated salmon with lemon dressing & chive oil

hot & sweet scallops with sticky rice & crab chopsticks

fillet of rabbit roasted in parma ham with fennel confit & chorizo oil

raspberry clafoutis in a sweet pastry box with a lemon sabayon

nick
nairn 138

hot smoked salmon with avocado salsa

a minestrone of shellfish

roast leg of lamb with garlic, rosemary, roasted baby plum tomatoes & broad bean "stew"

whisky parfait with agen prunes & earl grey syrup

james
martin 150

yorkshire pudding with foie gras & onion gravy

seared salmon with rice vermicelli

pan-fried, corn-fed breast of chicken with roasted ceps & jerusalem artichokes

panna cotta with spiced oranges

anton
edelmann 162

menu one 164

asparagus crown with crab

grilled irish salmon on minted pea purée with a red pepper jus

roast guinea fowl with a pistachio stuffing

marinated summer fruits & their soufflé

cheese petits fours:
chutney crunchies
cottage cheese tartlettes
goat's cheese crostini
brie tartlettes
brioche croûte with mango chutney and roquefort

anton
edelmann

menu two 176

canapés:
goat's cheese in a seed crust
gourmet delight
tuna tartare
scallop croûte with sauce vierge

smoked hock & goose liver terrine

courgette flower filled with seafood

roast fillet of beef with port-glazed shallots

peach melba & pineapple pot-pourri

paul&jeanne rankin 190

spiced aubergine soup with cumin flatbread

seared salmon with asian coleslaw & a soy-mustard vinaigrette

peppered duck breast with wild mushroom risotto cakes

catalan custard tart with a compote of oranges

cyrus todiwala 204

a plate of starters:
sheek kabab
(minced lamb with spices)
murghi na pattice
(spiced chicken and potato cakes)
duck tikka (duck in tandoori spices)
kanda bhajia (onion bhajia)

ullathiyad
(king prawn & scallops with fresh coconut, cumin & vegetables)

channa pulao
(chickpea spiced rice)

lagan nu custard
("Wedding Custard")

peter gordon 220

roast sweet potato, coconut & smoked paprika soup with goat's cheese wontons

grilled scallops with sweet chilli sauce & crème fraîche

roast lamb chump on kale & roast garlic polenta with pea & mint salsa

poached tamarillo with honey yoghurt bavarois & brandy snap

Inspired chefs 232

home-smoked salmon with tartare, hollandaise sauce & oriental dressing 234

Debbie Kelly-Greaves was inspired by Tony Tobin

oriental lamb salad with thai dressing 235

Darren O'Neil was inspired by Peter Gordon

chargrilled squid with a spicy coriander salad 236

John Whybrew was inspired by Franco Taruschio

seared beef salad with spiced beetroot & blue cheese dressing 236

Peader Daly was inspired by Paul and Jeanne Rankin

smoked chicken with avocado salsa, herb salad & pepper "paint" 238

Peter Joyner was inspired by Nick Nairn

cod with roasted glazed beetroot & garlic 239

Steve Holder was inspired by Paul Heathcote

roast rack of lamb with aubergine caviar 240

Andrew Gernon was inspired by Gary Rhodes

thai-style halibut with egg noodles 242

Mark Rees was inspired by Ross Burden

seared calves liver with red cabbage & savoury puy lentils 243

David Scott was inspired by Antony Worrall Thompson

pork rice paper parcels with sweet & sour coleslaw 244

Paul Burton was inspired by Ken Hom

saffron-scented sea bass with warm beetroot & potato salad 246

Malcolm Emery was inspired by Alastair Little

chicken kebab "methi murgh" 247

Michael Dornan was inspired by Cyrus Todiwala

roasted pear with vanilla ice cream & a chilli froth 249

Fiona Sweeting was inspired by James Martin

exotic fruit with a champagne sorbet 250

Andrew Scott was inspired by Anton Edelmann

Index 252

Credits 256

paulheathcote

At the age of 29 Paul opened his eponymous restaurant at Longridge, near Preston to much critical acclaim. Within two years he had been awarded his first Michelin and Egon Ronay stars along with *The Good Food Guide*'s 'Restaurant Of The Year' award. The 1994 Egon Ronay guide nominated Paul 'Chef Of The Year' and he earned his second Michelin star. Paul has gone on to open Heathcote's Brassiere in Preston and Simply Heathcotes in Manchester, together with Paul Heathcote's School of Excellence to help train aspiring chefs in the north of England. Paul Heathcote's early career took him from The Sharrow Bay Hotel via The Connaught Hotel to work alongside Raymond Blanc at Le Manoir aux Quat' Saisons. Paul has achieved all of this whilst developing a unique, distinctly British style of cuisine. His first cookery book, *Rhubarb and Black Pudding*, was completed with Matthew Fort.

paulheathcote

menu one

soup course

artichoke & foie gras soup

starter

seared salmon & poached egg
with watercress dressing

main course

fillet of beef with thyme, red wine &
root vegetables

dessert

rhubarb & elderflower omelette soufflé

Hopetoun House, Edinburgh

wines

white

Oyster Bay Sauvignon Blanc, Delegat's Estate 1999, New Zealand

A fine dry white with the freshness and assertive grassy aroma of a well made Sauvignon Blanc. The herbaceous nature of the wine and its crisp acidity provide a cleansing foil for the rich foie gras and artichoke soup.

Kleine Zalze Estate, Chardonnay, Coastal Region 1998, South Africa

A dry, full and buttery wine with a typically ripe "new world" style. The adaptable Chardonnay thrives in the warm South African climate to produce this flavoursome example, which provides plenty of flavour to match the richness of the salmon and egg in the salad.

red

Wente Estate Zinfandel 1998, California

A full-bodied red using California's "own" grape variety with fresh summer fruit flavours of damsons and strawberries. The weighty Zinfandel grape provides a fantastic quantity of fruit flavours, as well as plenty of youthful ripe tannins that are neutralised by the beef fats to provide a smooth, harmonious mouthfeel.

dessert

Botrytis Semillon-Sauvignon Blanc, Yalumba 1997, Australia

A glorious golden dessert wine, produced from late picked bunches of botrytised Semillon and Sauvignon Blanc grapes, with a luscious balance of richness, sugar and acidity. The hint of peach and apricot in the wine add to the fresh rhubarb and elderflower flavours, while the relatively light acidity is perfect for a dish containing eggs.

paulheathcote

artichoke & foie gras soup

25g (1oz) butter
1 onion, finely chopped
2 cloves garlic, crushed
2 globe artichokes, trimmed
1.2 litres (2 pints) chicken stock
50g (2oz) foie gras
150ml (1/4 pint) cream
bunch of fresh chives, snipped

Melt the butter in a heavy-based saucepan and sweat the onions, garlic and artichokes for 15 minutes, until softened. Cover with the stock and cook for a further 30 minutes. Liquidise the soup and pass through a sieve.

Divide the foie gras into 4 and briefly sear on each side in a hot pan. Pat dry with kitchen towels.

Add the cream, foie gras and chives to the warm soup and serve immediately.

seared salmon & poached egg with watercress dressing

olive oil, for frying
4 salmon fillets, each about 100g (4oz)
4 eggs
splash of vinegar, for poaching
selected leaves, to garnish

for the watercress dressing
3 tablespoons picked fresh tarragon
3 tablespoons picked fresh chervil
75g (3oz) picked watercress
1 teaspoon salt
2 tablespoons white wine vinegar
2 egg yolks
6 tablespoons vegetable oil

for the balsamic dressing
2 tablespoons balsamic vinegar
2 tablespoons red wine vinegar
6 tablespoons peanut oil
1 shallot, very finely chopped
1 clove garlic
1 teaspoon sugar
pinch of salt

First make the watercress dressing: blend the herbs, watercress, salt and wine vinegar into a paste. Add the egg yolks and blend well, then gradually add the oil. Blend until emulsified. Check for seasoning.

Mix together the ingredients for the balsamic dressing, strain and use to dress the leaves.

Heat the oil and pan-fry the salmon fillets until just done.

Poach the eggs in simmering water to which a splash of vinegar has been added.

To serve, place the salmon in the centre of each serving plate. Top with a poached egg and spoon over the watercress dressing. Garnish with the leaves.

fillet of beef with thyme, red wine & root vegetables

1 small swede

2 turnips

2 carrots

2 parsnips

500ml (15fl oz) chicken stock

450g (1lb) potatoes

50ml (2fl oz) milk

65g (2½oz) butter

1 tablespoon chopped fresh parsley

4 fillet steaks, each about 175g (6oz)

for the onion purée

1 onion, roughly chopped

150ml (¼ pint) whipping cream

salt and freshly ground black pepper

for the red wine sauce

250ml (8fl oz) red wine

1 shallot, roughly chopped

2 black peppercorns

few sprigs of fresh thyme

450ml (¾ pint) veal stock

Shape the swede, turnips, carrots and parsnips into barrel shapes. Lightly poach them in the chicken stock until tender. Drain, reserving a little of the poaching liquor.

To make the onion purée, place the onion in a pan and half cover with some of the reserved stock. Cover and cook gently, without colouring, until the onions are very soft. Strain the onions, return to the pan and place over a low heat to dry. Liquidise the onion until puréed. Bring the cream to the boil in a pan and heat until thickened and reduced by half. Add the puréed onion and season.

To make the red wine sauce, place the red wine, shallots, peppercorns and thyme in a pan and cook until reduced by three-quarters. Add the veal stock and cook until reduced to a sauce consistency, then pass through a sieve, discarding the solids.

Meanwhile, boil the potatoes in salted water until tender. Heat the milk and 40g (1½oz) of the butter and season to taste. Pour the milk and butter over the potatoes and mash until very smooth.

Just before serving, place the cooked root vegetables in a pan with the reserved poaching liquor, the rest of the butter and the chopped parsley, then reheat.

Cook the steaks to your liking then set aside to rest. To serve, pipe a neat cone of mashed potatoes on each plate. Next to this arrange the vegetables to form a bed for the steak, and arrange the steaks on top. Finish with a spoonful of onion purée as shown, then pour around the red wine sauce.

rhubarb & elderflower omelette soufflé

serves 6–8

450g (1lb) rhubarb, chopped
500ml (17fl oz) water

225g (8oz) sugar

icing sugar and fresh mint sprigs, to decorate

for the pancakes

1 egg

400ml (14fl oz) milk

2 tablespoons sugar

100g (4oz) flour

vegetable oil, for brushing pan

for the tuile baskets

30g (1 1/4oz) flour

50g (2oz) icing sugar

2 egg whites

25g (1oz) butter, melted

for the sauce anglaise

1 vanilla pod, seeds scraped out

5 tablespoons cream

150ml (1/4 pint) milk

40g (1 1/2oz) sugar

3 egg yolks, whisked

for the poached rhubarb

3 tablespoons Port

75g (3oz) sugar

350g (12oz) rhubarb, sliced

for the soufflé

250ml (8fl oz) milk

2 tablespoons elderflower cordial

75g (3oz) sugar

3 egg yolks

15g (1/2oz) cornflour

1 egg white

First make the rhubarb sorbet: put the rhubarb, water and sugar into a saucepan. Bring to the boil, then simmer until the rhubarb is tender. Blend and sieve. Freeze in an ice cream machine.

To make the pancakes, whisk the egg, milk and sugar together. Slowly pour the egg mixture into the flour, whisk, and sieve. Brush a small non-stick pan with oil, heat and add a spoonful of the pancake mixture. Cook until golden on both sides.

To make the tuile baskets, preheat the oven to 160°C/325°F/Gas Mark 3. Sift together the flour and icing sugar. Slowly mix in the egg whites, then the butter. Line a large baking sheet with greaseproof paper. Spread a spoonful of the mixture thinly over the paper. Bake for 5–6 minutes, until light brown. While warm, mould over an upturned ramekin dish to form a cup.

To make the sauce anglaise, add the vanilla seeds to the cream, milk and sugar. Bring to the boil. Slowly whisk the mixture into the egg yolks. Return the mixture to the pan and cook, stirring, until it reaches a sauce consistency. Sieve and chill.

Meanwhile, poach the rhubarb. Bring the Port and sugar to the boil. Add the rhubarb and poach for 4 minutes, until tender. Drain.

To make the soufflé, bring the milk and cordial to the boil. Whisk 25g (1oz) of the sugar with the egg yolks. Add the cornflour to the sugar mixture, and slowly whisk in the milk. Place in a clean pan and cook until thickened, then sieve and allow to cool. Whisk the remaining sugar with the egg white until it forms soft peaks, then carefully fold it into the elderflower mixture. Fold in the poached rhubarb. Spoon the soufflé over one half of each pancake. Fold the pancake over to encase the soufflé and bake in an oven preheated to 190°C/375°F/Gas Mark 5 for 5 minutes, until golden and risen.

Place a ball of sorbet in each tuile basket and serve with a soufflé pancake and sauce anglaise. Decorate with icing sugar and mint.

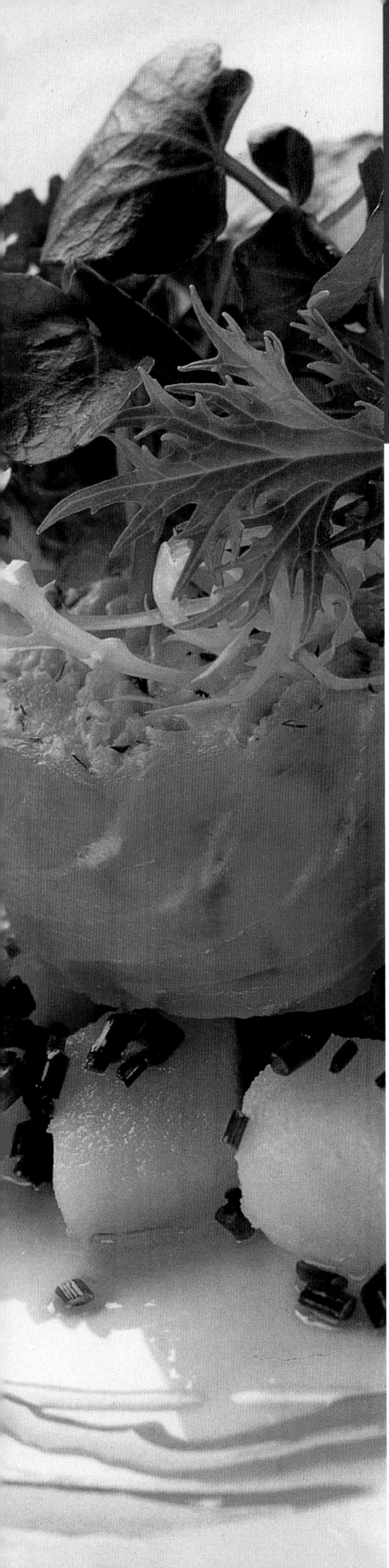

paulheathcote

menu two

appetizer

potted salmon with potato salad,
soured cream & chive oil

main course

steamed guinea fowl with mash, artichokes,
asparagus & yellow wine sauce

dessert

raspberry & pistachio brûlée
with raspberry sorbet

Kenley House, Surrey

wines

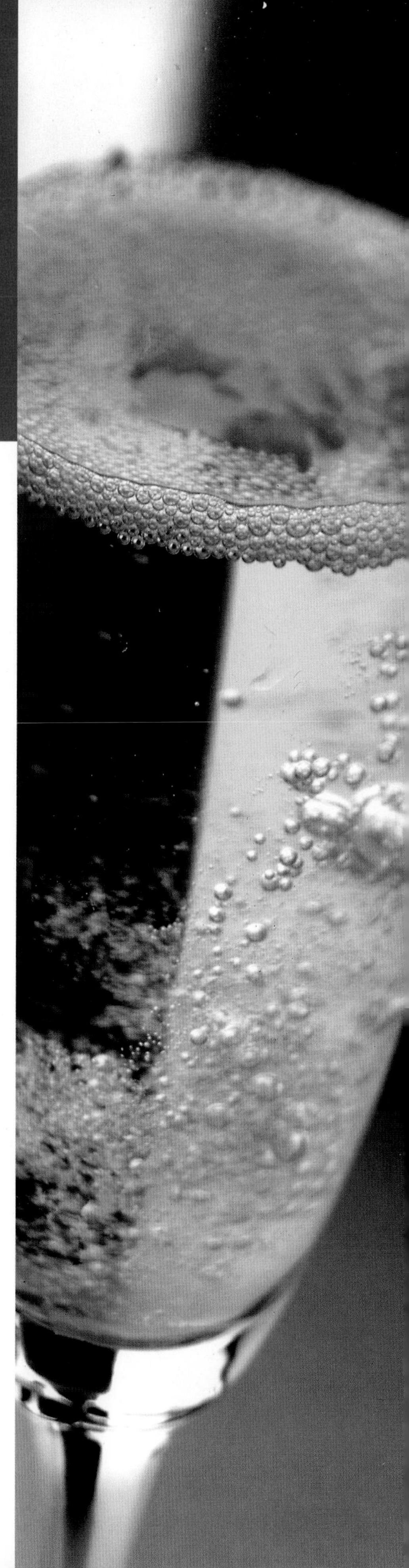

white

Evans & Tate Gnangara Chardonnay-Verdhelho 1998, Australia

An unoaked blend of 55 per cent Chardonnay and 45 per cent Verdelho (a successful Portuguese import that thrives in a hot climate). The wine exhibits excellent tropical fruit aromas, with a crisp acidity typical of Western Australian whites. Its full-flavoured palate competes well with the spicy potted salmon and fresh chive flavours.

red

Fetzer Pinot Noir 1997, California

A soft, easy-drinking wine with spicy, ripe, redcurrant and vanilla flavours on the nose and palate. Ageing in new French oak adds a rounded, buttery taste to the finish. Pinot Noir, the grape of red Burgundy, is a great match for many medium to strongly flavoured game bird dishes, with its light tannins and juicy red fruit flavours.

dessert

Château Malagar, Moelleux, D. Cordier 1997, France

Made from 60 per cent Semillon and 40 per cent Sauvignon Blanc just across the river from the prestigious Sauternes appellation, this wine is typical of the region. Luscious and sweet with hints of apricot and peaches from being Botrytis-affected, it is a classic dessert wine that will complement the raspberries and pistachios without being too cloying.

potted salmon with potato salad, soured cream & chive oil

100ml ($3^1/_2$fl oz) creamed horseradish

1 leaf of gelatine, soaked

1 shallot, finely chopped and blanched

3 tablespoons chopped fresh dill

5 green peppercorns, finely chopped

$^1/_2$ clove garlic, crushed

1 tablespoon lemon juice

350g (12oz) salmon, poached in fish stock and chilled

salt and freshly ground black pepper

100g (4oz) smoked salmon, thinly sliced

4 tablespoons soured cream

mixed salad leaves, to garnish

for the chive oil

150ml ($^1/_4$ pint) extra-virgin olive oil

25g (1oz) chives

for the potato salad

450g (1lb) Maris Piper potatoes, peeled and cut into 1cm ($^1/_2$in) dice

2 tablespoons snipped fresh chives

3 tablespoons olive oil

First make the chive oil: place the oil and chives in a food processor and liquidise for 2 minutes. Season to taste and pass the mixture through a fine sieve. Set the oil aside.

Warm the creamed horseradish and add the gelatine. When the gelatine has dissolved, mix in the shallot, dill, peppercorns, garlic, lemon juice and the flaked poached salmon. Season to taste.

Lay out the thin slices of smoked salmon on a sheet of plastic film. Place the poached salmon mixture on the smoked salmon and roll up like a "sausage roll", then refrigerate.

Boil the potatoes until tender but still firm, then refresh in cold water. Drain, season, and add the snipped chives and olive oil. Toss until the potatoes are coated in the chives and oil.

Remove the plastic film and cut the salmon roll into 2.5cm (1in) thick slices. To serve, place the salmon roll on a bed of potatoes, drizzle a little soured cream and chive oil around and arrange the salad leaves on top of the salmon, to garnish.

paulheathcote

steamed guinea fowl with mash, artichokes, asparagus & yellow wine sauce

2 guinea fowl, legs removed and roughly chopped, breasts reserved

12 spears asparagus, trimmed, blanched and refreshed

450g (1lb) potatoes, peeled and cubed

50ml (2fl oz) milk

60g ($2^1/2$oz) butter

4 baby artichokes, outer leaves removed and inner leaves trimmed

freshly ground black pepper

chives, cut into 2.5cm (1in) lengths, to garnish

truffle oil, for drizzling

for the yellow wine sauce

30ml (1fl oz) olive oil

1 shallot, finely sliced

½ stick of celery, roughly chopped

1 bay leaf

1 sprig of fresh tarragon

6 white peppercorns, crushed

1 clove garlic, left whole

25g (1oz) button mushrooms, finely sliced

10g (⅓oz) dried morels, soaked in warm water, strained and finely chopped

1 glass Jura Yellow wine

150ml (¼ pint) light chicken stock

150ml (¼ pint) whipping cream

salt

lemon juice to taste

First make the yellow wine sauce: heat the oil in a pan. Add the chopped guinea fowl legs, shallots, celery, bay leaf, tarragon, peppercorns, garlic and button mushrooms and sauté over a low heat for about 5 minutes.

Add the morels and sauté for a further 30 seconds before adding the wine. Continue to cook until reduced by half, then add the chicken stock.

Reduce by a third, then add the cream. Cook for about 30 minutes until a thin sauce consistency. Pass through a sieve and season with salt and lemon juice.

To make the mash, boil the potatoes in salted water until tender. Heat the milk and 25g (1oz) of the butter, and season to taste. Pour it over the potatoes and mash until very smooth.

Cook the artichokes in boiling water until tender. Leave to cool, then halve or quarter. Pan-fry in 25g (1oz) of the butter until slightly browned.

Make a few criss-cross incisions on the undersides of the guinea fowl breasts and season with salt and pepper. Roll out a piece of plastic film and place some of the remaining butter on it, put one breast on top and roll up very tightly, twist the end of the film and tie. Repeat with the remaining breasts. Steam for 10–12 minutes in the plastic film. Allow to rest for 2 minutes.

Remove the plastic film, retaining the juices for the sauce. Cut the breasts into half diagonally.

Just before serving, use a hand blender to froth up the yellow wine sauce. Place the guinea fowl on a bed of mashed potato with the artichokes and asparagus, and pour on a little yellow wine sauce. Garnish with chives and drizzle with truffle oil.

raspberry & pistachio brûlée with raspberry sorbet

200ml (7fl oz) double cream mixed with 200ml (7fl oz) whipping cream

24 raspberries

75g (3oz) caster sugar

1 vanilla pod, split and seeds scraped out

75g (3oz) pistachio paste

5 egg yolks

brown sugar, for sprinkling

raspberries, for decoration

for the raspberry sorbet

725g (1¾lb) raspberries

375g (13oz) sugar

375ml (13fl oz) water

for the chocolate tuiles (makes 24 – keep unused tuiles in an airtight tin)

100g (4oz) unsalted butter

100g (4oz) icing sugar

½ teaspoon vanilla extract

3 egg whites

85g (3¼oz) flour, sifted

15g (½oz) cocoa powder, sifted

First make the raspberry sorbet: put all the ingredients into a pan and bring to the boil until the sugar has dissolved. Liquidise the mixture, then pass through a fine sieve. Cool, then place in an ice cream machine and follow the manufacturer's instructions.

To make the chocolate tuiles, preheat the oven to 200°C/400°F/Gas Mark 6. Cream the butter, sugar and vanilla extract in a bowl. Gradually beat in the egg whites, then fold in the flour and cocoa powder until you have a smooth paste. Leave to chill for about 2 hours.

Place small spoonfuls of the tuiles mixture about 10cm (4in) apart on a non-stick baking sheet, then spread into rounds with a spatula. Bake for about 4 minutes, until the mixture is just beginning to colour – keep checking. Remove the baking sheet from the oven and leave to cool very slightly until you can handle the tuiles. Lift each tuile off the baking sheet with a palette knife and drape over a dariole mould or upturned cup to form a basket shape. Leave until cool and set, then lift off gently.

To make the brûlée, reserve a quarter of the cream and chill until required. Place the raspberries in the bottom of 4 ramekin dishes.

Mix the remaining cream with the sugar, vanilla pod and seeds and the pistachio paste. Heat the mixture in a heavy-based saucepan until just below boiling point, making sure the sugar has dissolved and the pistachio paste has been incorporated. Leave to cool for 5 minutes, then remove the vanilla pod.

Whisk the cream mixture into the egg yolks and add the remaining chilled cream. Pour the mixture over the raspberries in the ramekins and bake in an oven preheated to 110°C/225°F/Gas Mark ¼ for 45–60 minutes, until just set.

Preheat the grill to high. Sprinkle brown sugar over the ramekins to cover and heat under the grill until caramelised. Allow to cool for 20 minutes before serving.

Place a spoonful of the raspberry sorbet in a tuile basket and serve with a pistachio brûlée, decorated with a few raspberries.

francotaruschio

Franco Taruschio has been the owner/proprietor of the Walnut Tree Inn, Abergavenny since 1963. Over the years Franco and his wife, Ann, have built up a solid and loyal customer base. The Walnut Tree Inn can easily lay claim to be one of the very best Italian restaurants in Britain, offering superb food in comfortable and relaxed surroundings. The Taruschios have published many recipe books including *Leaves From the Walnut Tree*, *Bruschetta, Crostoni and Crostini*, and *Franco & Friends – Food From The Walnut Tree* which accompanied the BBC television series.

francotaruschio

menu

appetizer

panzerotti fritti (deep-fried mozzarella pastries)

starter

vincisgrassi (an 18th-century pasta dish – pasta and béchamel sauce enriched with Parma ham, porcini mushrooms and truffle)

fish course

crocchette d'eglesino affumicato con salsa d'aragosta (smoked haddock fishcakes with lobster bisque sauce)

main course

quaglie arrosto con salvia e frittedda (roast quail with sage, and braised spring vegetables)

dessert

trio of coffee desserts:

panna cotta al caffè (coffee-flavoured mascarpone custard)

crema bruciata di caffè (coffee crème brûlée)

gelato al caffè con salsa di caffè (coffee ice cream with coffee sauce)

RAF Museum, Cosford

wines

white

Pinot Grigio del Veneto, Linea Corte Vigna 1998, Italy

Dry, delicately flavoured wine, with a peach and almond fruit character and a racy acidity. An ideal partner for the rich Vincisgrassi, with its béchamel sauce and lightly flavoured Parma ham. The wine successfully manages to cut through the sauce without overpowering the delicate flavours and delivers a complementary hint of peach and nuts.

Riesling, Steinacker, Cave Vinicole de Ribeauvillé 1998, France

A wine exhibiting elegance and finesse. It has a dry, steely almost minerally quality with a fantastic lime acidity on the finish, which forms a lovely contrast to the fish course: the acidity cutting through the rich lobster bisque and the lime character perfectly adding to the haddock fishcakes.

red

Salice Salentino Riserva, Taurino 1996, Italy

The leading producer in Apulia makes a beautiful harmonious wine with rich game, spice and oak flavours lingering on the palate. This is a powerful red with velvety fruit matched by strong, dry tannins, and is therefore quite well equipped to stand up to the richness of the quail and pancetta, as well as the braised spring vegetables.

dessert

Late Harvest Orange Muscat and Flora, Brown Brothers 1999, Australia

A luscious dessert wine made from a rare blend of two grape varieties grown in Victoria. It has a wonderfully light, floral aroma and sweet grapey palate. It also shows more than a hint of orange fruit character, generally a great match with chocolate and coffee.

francotaruschio

panzerotti fritti

serves 4–6

These tasty morsels are served as an appetizer with pre-dinner drinks. If you are short of time, wonton wrappers can be used instead of the pasta dough. Seal the wrappers with beaten egg and deep-fry in the same way for a light, crisp result.

for the pastry

200g (7oz) plain flour

100g (3½oz) butter, diced

1 egg yolk

2 tablespoons milk

salt

for the filling

200g (7oz) mozzarella, finely diced

50g (1¾oz) Parma ham, cut in julienne

30g (1oz) Parmesan, freshly grated

2 eggs

a good pinch of finely chopped parsley

a small pinch of freshly grated nutmeg

salt and freshly ground black pepper

to finish

1 egg beaten with a few drops of water, for the egg wash

light olive oil, for deep-frying

salt

To make the pastry dough, put the flour into a bowl and make a hollow in the centre. Add the butter, egg yolk, milk and salt to the hollow. Work the ingredients together with your fingertips to make a dough. Cover the bowl with a cloth and leave the dough to rest at room temperature for 30 minutes.

Roll out the pastry dough on a floured board into an oblong shape. Fold the dough twice back on itself, then cover again and leave once more for 30 minutes.

Mix together the ingredients for the filling.

Roll out the pastry dough until 3mm (⅛in) thick. Cut it into two equal pieces. Brush one sheet with the egg wash. Dot blobs of the filling in rows on the egg-washed sheet, leaving a space of 3cm (1¼in) between the blobs. Brush the second sheet of pastry with egg wash and lay it over the first sheet, egg-washed side down. Using a finger, press down around the blobs of filling, then cut into squares or oblongs using a pastry wheel. Press with a finger all around the edges to ensure the *panzerotti* are well sealed. Put the *panzerotti* on a floured cloth as they are prepared.

Brush the *panzerotti* with egg wash, then deep-fry in hot olive oil for about 6 minutes, turning to cook and colour evenly. Drain on kitchen paper and serve at once, sprinkled with salt.

vincisgrassi

serves 6

This is a speciality of the Marche region of Italy, in particular of Macerata. The story goes that the dish was named after an Austrian general, Windisch Graetz, who was with his troops in Ancona in 1799 during the Napoleonic war. Actually Antonio Nebbia, who wrote a gastronomic manual in 1784, mentioned in his book a similar dish called Princisgras.

for the pasta

500g (1lb 2oz) farina O or strong plain flour

2 whole eggs, plus 4 egg yolks

1 teaspoon salt

for the sauce

150g (5oz) butter

60g (2oz) flour

1.2 litres (2 pints) milk

400g (14oz) porcini, sliced

60ml (2fl oz) extra-virgin olive oil

200g (7oz) Parma ham, cut into julienne

200ml (7fl oz) single cream

3 tablespoons finely chopped parsley

salt and freshly ground black pepper

150g (5oz) freshly grated Parmesan cheese

truffle oil, or if possible a little shaved white truffle

Make a dough from the pasta ingredients, knead well and roll through a pasta machine as you would for lasagne. Cut the pasta lengths into squares, approximately 12.5cm (5in) square. Cook the squares in plenty of boiling salted water, a few at a time. Place on linen cloths to drain.

For the sauce, melt 50g (2oz) of the butter, add the flour and blend in well. Add the milk, which has been previously heated, a little at a time, beating well with a balloon whisk.

Cook the porcini in the olive oil and add to the béchamel. Stir in the Parma ham. Add the cream and parsley, season, and bring to the boil. Turn off the heat.

To assemble the vincisgrassi, butter a gratin dish and cover the bottom with a layer of pasta, then spread over a layer of béchamel, dot with butter and sprinkle with some Parmesan cheese. Continue the process, making layer after layer, finishing with a béchamel layer and a sprinkling of Parmesan cheese. Cook in an oven preheated to 220°C/425°F/ Gas Mark 7 for 20 minutes.

Serve with a little truffle oil splashed on top or, better still, with shavings of white truffle, and a little Parmesan cheese.

crocchette d'eglesino affumicato con salsa d'aragosta

225g (8oz) potatoes, such as Maris Piper, peeled and quartered

450g (1lb) smoked haddock

300ml (½ pint milk)

1 egg yolk

salt and freshly ground black pepper

chilli powder, to taste

50g (2oz) plain flour, seasoned

1 egg, beaten

100g (4oz) breadcrumbs

vegetable oil, for frying

fresh flat-leaf parsley, to garnish

for the lobster bisque sauce

4 tablespoons olive oil

shells of 2 boiled lobsters

2 tablespoons brandy

100g (4oz) carrots, finely chopped

50g (2oz) leeks, finely sliced

50g (2oz) celery sticks, finely chopped

2 cloves garlic, chopped

2 tomatoes, diced

1 bay leaf

50g (2oz) tomato purée

250ml (8fl oz) double cream

First make the lobster bisque sauce: heat 2 tablespoons of the oil in a saucepan and when very hot add the lobster shells, then fry for 5 minutes. Add the brandy and allow to ignite, then remove from the heat and reserve.

Heat the remaining oil in a frying pan, add the carrots, leeks, celery, and garlic and fry for a few minutes, then add the tomatoes and cook until the tomatoes have become pulpy.

Combine the vegetable mixture and lobster shells and add enough water to cover the mixture. Add the bay leaf and stir in the tomato purée. Bring to the boil, reduce the heat, and simmer the mixture for 45 minutes, skimming away any froth that forms.

Line a sieve with muslin and strain the sauce. Return the sauce to a small pan, and season with salt. Add the cream and cook until reduced and slightly thickened. Set aside.

To make the fishcakes, boil the potatoes for 15 minutes, until tender, then drain and mash.

Poach the haddock in the milk until just cooked. Flake the fish, removing any bones, and combine with the potato. Add the egg yolk, seasoning and a little chilli to taste, then mix to combine.

Using your hands, shape the mixture into individual fishcakes, each one about 100g (4oz). Dip each cake into the seasoned flour, the beaten egg and then the breadcrumbs, to coat. Heat the oil in a large frying pan. Fry the fishcakes until golden on both sides. Serve the fishcakes with the sauce, garnished with parsley.

francotaruschio

quaglie arrosto con salvia e frittedda

4 plump quails

salt and freshly ground black pepper

4 sprigs of fresh sage

50g (2oz) butter

4 slices streaky bacon

Salt and pepper the quails, stuff each one with a sprig of sage and put a little butter inside each cavity. Spread the rest of the butter on the breasts and legs of the birds.

Wrap the streaky bacon around each bird, making sure the thighs of the bird are covered.

Place the quails in a roasting tin and roast in an oven set at 200°C/400°F/Gas Mark 6 for 15 minutes.

Remove the birds from the roasting tin and serve the quails with the *frittedda* (braised spring vegetables) below.

frittedda

6 tender purple globe artichokes (viola or spinosi)

lemon juice

1kg (2¼lb) fresh young broad beans

500g (1lb 2oz) fresh peas

1 small onion, finely chopped

3 tablespoons extra-virgin olive oil

salt and freshly ground black pepper

freshly grated nutmeg

3 tablespoons dry white wine

½ teaspoon sugar

12 fresh mint leaves, chopped

Prepare the artichokes by removing the hard outer leaves and trimming off the stalk, leaving about 5cm (2in) attached to the artichoke. Peel the stalk and trim round the base of the artichoke. Cut off the tips of the artichoke leaves straight across with a sharp knife. Cut each artichoke lengthways into 5 segments and drop into water acidulated with lemon juice.

Shell the broad beans and peas. If there are any large beans among the broad beans, always remove the outer skins.

Fry the onion in the olive oil in a saucepan until light gold. Add the artichoke segments, well drained. Stir them well into the onion and oil mixture, then add a ladle of water. Add the beans and peas to the pan. Season with salt, pepper and a little grating of nutmeg. Leave to cook over a low heat, stirring occasionally and adding a little more water if necessary.

When the artichokes are tender, add the wine, sugar and mint. Mix well and cook for a further 2–3 minutes. Serve immediately with the quail or leave to cool.

Il mare colore del vino
91

francotaruschio

trio of coffee desserts:

panna cotta al caffè

Serve this dessert with the gelato al caffè (coffee ice cream) on page 41, and crema bruciata di caffè (crème brûlée) opposite, as part of a trio of coffee desserts. A little coffee sauce (see page 41) adds the finishing touch.

serves 4–6

170g (6oz) caster sugar

juice of ½ lemon

225g (8oz) mascarpone

400ml (14fl oz) milk

2 teaspoons instant espresso coffee powder

10g (⅓oz) powdered gelatine

Put half the sugar, the lemon juice and 4 tablespoons water into a heavy-based saucepan and dissolve over a low heat, stirring every now and then. Do not allow the water to boil before the sugar has dissolved. In the meantime, heat 4–6 ramekins in a warm oven.

When the syrup is quite clear, bring it to a gentle boil and, without stirring, let it turn a golden colour. Be careful it does not burn.

Remove the ramekins from the oven and pour in the caramel, tipping the dishes to coat the sides and bottom completely. Be careful as you are dealing with very hot caramel. Set the dishes aside.

In the saucepan in which the caramel was cooked, combine the mascarpone, milk, coffee powder and remaining sugar. Bring the mixture slowly to the boil, whisking with a balloon whisk to break up the mascarpone. Remove the pan from the heat and leave the mixture to cool and infuse for 1 hour.

In a cup, soften the gelatine in 4 tablespoons of water. Set the cup in a pan of hot water and stir until the gelatine is completely dissolved and clear. Stir briskly into the mascarpone mixture. Pour the mixture into the caramel-coated ramekins and refrigerate until firm.

To serve, invert each ramekin onto a plate and shake the *panna cotta* loose.

pictured on page 40

crema bruciata di caffè

serves 8

1 large egg plus 6 large egg yolks

120g (4oz) granulated sugar

400ml (14fl oz) double cream

400ml (14fl oz) milk

1 1/2 tablespoons instant espresso coffee powder

2 tablespoons Tia Maria or Kahlua

45g (1 1/2 oz) soft light brown sugar

Preheat the oven to 170°C/325°F/gas 3. In a bowl whisk together the whole egg, egg yolks and sugar.

Heat the cream and milk in a heavy saucepan until just boiling. Add the espresso coffee powder and liqueur and stir until the powder is dissolved.

Pour the cream mixture into the egg mixture in a stream, whisking constantly. Skim off any froth.

Divide the custard among 8 ramekins or heatproof cups and set them in a baking tray. Pour enough hot water into the tray to reach half-way up the sides of the ramekins. Bake the custards in the middle of the oven for about 40 minutes, or until just set and trembling. Leave the custards to cool, then chill for at least 4 hours.

Cover the tops of the custards with an even layer of brown sugar and caramelize with a blowtorch.

pictured on page 40

gelato al caffè con salsa di caffè

serves 6

5 egg yolks

200g (7oz) caster sugar

350ml (12fl oz) milk

3 tablespoons espresso coffee

coffee sauce, to serve (see below)

Whisk the egg yolks and sugar in a large bowl until creamy. Bring the milk to the boil in a heavy saucepan, and gradually pour it on to the egg mixture. Stir in the coffee.

Return the mixture to the saucepan and place over a moderate heat. Stir with a wooden spoon until the mixture thickens enough to coat the back of the spoon.

Remove from the heat and cool quickly, then freeze in an ice cream machine according to the manufacturer's instructions.

To serve, pour a little coffee sauce onto individual plates and spoon the ice-cream on top.

salsa di caffè

300ml (1/2 pint) milk

3 teaspoons instant espresso coffee powder

3 egg yolks

60g (2oz) caster sugar

Mix the milk with the coffee powder, then heat until boiling.

In a bowl, beat the egg yolks and sugar together until light and creamy. Pour the heated milk on to the egg mixture, stirring all the time. Return the sauce to a clean saucepan and cook over a gentle heat, stirring, until thickened.

Serve with the coffee ice cream.

trio of coffee desserts shown clockwise, from left:

gelato al caffè con salsa di caffè, crema bruciata di caffè (recipe page 39), panna cotta al caffè (recipe page 38)

rossburden

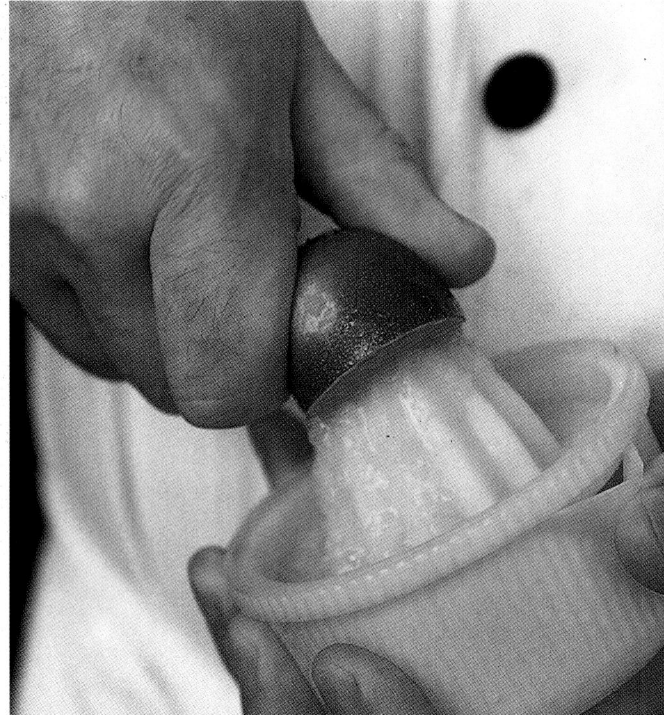

Ross Burden was born in New Zealand and moved to England in 1990. His no-nonsense approach to food and entertaining has gained him many fans. Ross is a veteran on BBC's *Ready, Steady Cook* and has hosted his own show for Carlton Food Network. His love of travel is reflected in the diversity of his cooking repertoire, drawing influences from Italy, Thailand and beyond. Ross passionately believes in cooking with fresh seasonal ingredients. His only rule is that food should be fun and shared with friends.

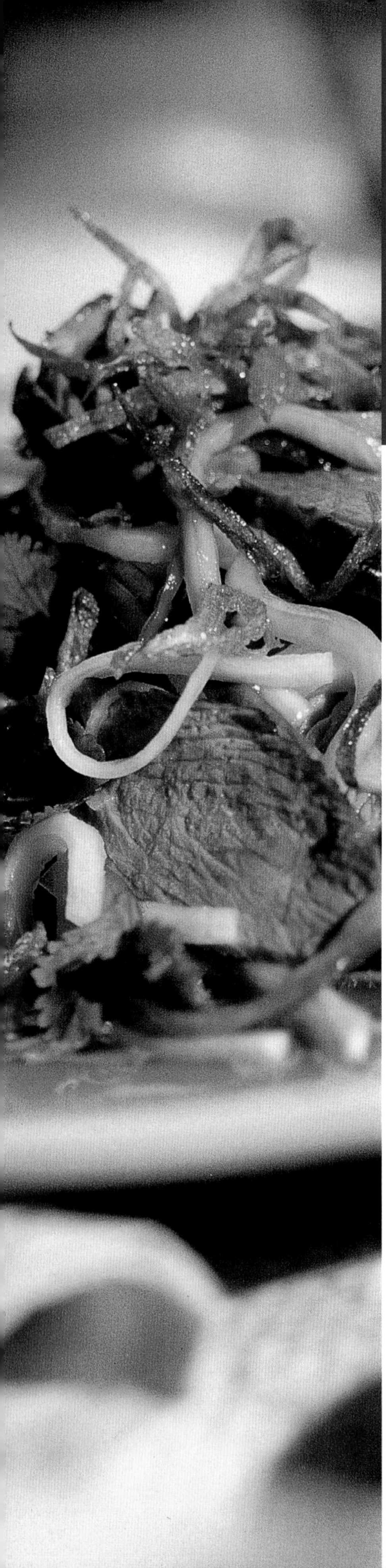

rossburden

menu

appetizer

salad of kangaroo fillet with crispy shallots

fish course

thai fishcakes with dipping sauce

main course

steamed halibut steaks with garlic oil

pad thai

dessert

coconut tart with raspberry sauce, star anise ice cream & maraschino sabayon

Highclere Castle, Hampshire

wines

red

Pinot Noir, 'Vieilles Vignes', J. Kentzinger 1997, France

A light, pale Pinot Noir with a delicious strawberry fragrance. Made from low yielding vines and aged briefly in oak barrels. The key here is to match the dark kangaroo meat with a red that will not overpower the dish and the rest of the menu. Pinot Noir is perfect as it is one of the lighter red grapes, yet commands good fruit flavours.

white

Sauvignon Blanc, Vidal Estate 1998, New Zealand

A classic crisp, gooseberry grassy style of Sauvignon Blanc mingled with passion fruit and melon flavours. A complex wine with great intensity and length, from the Hawkes Bay area of the North Island. Another grape that generally produces a crisp, dry wine. The herbaceous nature of the fruit flavours will certainly enhance the fishcakes.

Moselland Classic Riesling Kabinett, Wiltinger Scharzberg 1998, Germany

From the Saar region, a tributary of the Mosel, noted for producing a delicate style. It has a wonderful racy lime acidity and the classic steely, minerally, Riesling fruit character. The underrated grape variety Riesling is a cracking match with most fish, and here the citrussy acidity easily counters the richness of the garlic oil which accompanies the halibut, cleansing the palate.

rossburden

salad of kangaroo fillet with crispy shallots

500g (1lb 2oz) kangaroo fillet or rump or fillet steak, trimmed of sinew and fat

200g (7oz) mooli, cut into julienne

200g (7oz) carrots, cut into julienne

200g (7oz) cucumber, cut into julienne

1 bunch spring onions, shredded, green parts put in iced water to curl

1 handful fresh coriander leaves

coriander roots from above, very finely sliced

4 fresh kaffir lime leaves, finely shredded

2 bird's eye chillies, cut into julienne

4 shallots (preferably Thai pink), finely sliced and fried until golden

for the dressing

2 tablespoons lime juice

2 tablespoons fish sauce

2 teaspoons brown (or palm) sugar

1/4 teaspoon white pepper

2 teaspoons sesame oil

Preheat the oven to 200°C/400°F/ Gas Mark 6. Sear the kangaroo fillet on both sides in a frying pan for 2 minutes, until browned. Place in a roasting dish and roast for 10 minutes. Remove from the oven, cover, and leave to rest. Slice the kangaroo into strips.

Mix together the ingredients for the dressing.

Combine the mooli, carrots, cucumber, spring onions, coriander, kaffir lime leaves and chillies in a bowl, then pour the dressing over. Mix to coat the salad in the dressing.

Pile the salad on 4 serving plates, top with the sliced kangaroo and sprinkle with the crispy shallots. Serve immediately.

thai fishcakes with dipping sauce

5 dried red chillies, halved and deseeded

1 shallot, finely sliced

2 cloves garlic, roughly chopped

2 coriander roots, chopped

1 teaspoon finely chopped galangal

6 fresh kaffir lime leaves, finely chopped

pinch of salt

450g (1lb) cod, or other white fish, skinned and finely chopped

½ teaspoon fish sauce

50g (2oz) fine green beans, sliced very finely

vegetable oil, for deep-frying

chillies and cucumber, to garnish

for the dipping sauce

150ml (¼ pint) rice vinegar

150g (5oz) caster sugar

3 red chillies, finely sliced

First make the dipping sauce: put the vinegar and sugar in a saucepan and bring to the boil. Cook for 2–3 minutes, until syrupy. Stir in the chillies, then leave to cool.

To prepare the fishcakes, pound the chillies, shallot, garlic, coriander roots, galangal, kaffir lime leaves and salt in a mortar to make a thick, coarse paste.

Place the paste in a mixing bowl and, using your fingers, blend thoroughly with the fish (or blend in a food processor). Add the fish sauce and the green beans and knead until combined.

Shape the mixture into small, flat cakes, about 5cm (2in) diameter and 1cm (½in) thick.

Heat a pan of oil for deep frying to 200°C/400°F. Deep-fry the cakes for 2–3 minutes, until golden brown on both sides. Drain on kitchen towels.

Serve the fishcakes warm, decorated with chilli flowers and cucumber, and accompanied by the dipping sauce.

rossburden

steamed halibut steaks with garlic oil

4 halibut steaks, each about 175g (6oz)

5cm (2in) piece of fresh ginger, finely sliced

6 spring onions, white part sliced, green part shredded, placed in iced water to curl

2½ tablespoons soy sauce

2½ tablespoons sesame oil

4 tablespoons mirin

3 cloves garlic, sliced

4 tablespoons oil

Place the halibut steaks on a plate in a steamer. Arrange the ginger and the white part of the spring onions over the fish. Sprinkle the soy sauce, sesame oil and mirin over the fish, then steam for 8 minutes until the fish is opaque.

Meanwhile, fry the sliced garlic in oil until it is very crisp but not burnt. Strain the garlic, reserving the oil. To serve, pour the hot oil over the cooked fish and garnish with the garlic slices and the spring onions.

pad thai

6 tablespoons sunflower oil

3 cloves garlic, finely chopped

2 eggs

250g (9oz) Chinese egg noodles, soaked in water until soft, then drained

4 tablespoons lemon juice

3 tablespoons fish sauce

3 teaspoons sugar

4 tablespoons chopped roasted cashews

1 teaspoon chilli powder

2 tablespoons finely chopped preserved radish (mooli)

50g (2oz) beansprouts

4 spring onions, sliced into 2.5cm (1in pieces)

2 sprigs of fresh coriander, coarsely chopped

lemon wedges, to garnish

Heat the oil in a wok or frying pan, add the garlic and fry until golden brown. Break the eggs into the wok, cook for a couple of seconds, stirring vigorously. Add the noodles and stir well, scraping down the sides of the wok to mix the noodles with the egg.

Add to the pan the lemon juice, fish sauce, sugar, half the cashews, the chilli powder, preserved radish, 1 tablespoon of the beansprouts and the spring onions. Toss and stir the mixture until all the ingredients are thoroughly combined.

Test the noodles for tenderness. When cooked, turn on to a large serving plate. Arrange the remaining cashews and beansprouts around the dish. Garnish with the coriander and lemon wedges and serve.

coconut tart with raspberry sauce, star anise ice cream & maraschino sabayon

serves 8

2 eggs

grated zest of 2 lemons

200g (7oz) caster sugar

375ml (13fl oz) double cream

juice of 2 lemons

225g (8oz) desiccated coconut

sprigs of fresh mint, to decorate

for the pastry

350g (12oz) plain flour

pinch of salt

75g (3oz) icing sugar

175g (6oz) unsalted butter, cut into small pieces

2 eggs

for the raspberry sauce

300g (10½oz) raspberries

50g (2oz) caster sugar

juice of ½ lemon

star anise ice cream & maraschino sabayon, to serve (recipe page 54)

First make the pastry case: sift the flour, salt and sugar into a bowl. Add the butter and rub with your fingertips until the mixture forms fine breadcrumbs. Make a well in the centre of the mixture, then add the eggs and mix with a knife to form crumbs. Press the crumbs together with your fingers. Knead lightly for a few seconds, then form into a ball. Wrap with cling film and leave to rest in the refrigerator for 30 minutes.

Roll out the dough and use to line a 25cm (10in) tart tin, with removable base, then chill for about 20 minutes, until firm.

Preheat the oven to 200°C/400°F/ Gas Mark 6. Prick the base of the dough, line with greaseproof paper, and partly fill with baking beans. Bake for 10–15 minutes, until the pastry is lightly browned. Remove the beans and paper.

Reduce the oven to 160°C/325°F/ Gas Mark 3. Mix together the eggs, lemon zest and sugar. Gently mix in the cream, then the lemon juice and finally the desiccated coconut. Pour the cream mixture into the pastry shell and bake for about 40 minutes, until golden. Leave to cool for about 1 hour.

To make the raspberry sauce, put the raspberries, sugar and lemon juice in a saucepan. Bring to the boil together, then whisk, and pass through a sieve.

Cut the coconut tart into slices and serve with a ball of the star anise ice cream. Drizzle around the raspberry sauce and maraschino sabayon. Decorate with a sprig of fresh mint.

rossburden

star anise ice cream & maraschino sabayon

300ml (1/2 pint) double cream

300ml (1/2 pint) whole milk

1 vanilla pod, split lengthways

6 star anise

200g (7oz) caster sugar

10 egg yolks

for the maraschino sabayon

2 egg yolks

60g (2 1/4oz) caster sugar

2 tablespoons maraschino liqueur

First make the ice cream: put the cream, milk, vanilla pod, star anise and half the sugar in a heavy saucepan and bring almost to the boil. Beat the yolks with the rest of the sugar in a bowl. Pour the hot cream mixture over the egg yolk mixture and stir to combine, then return it to the pan.

Cook briefly over a low heat, stirring, until thickened. Discard the vanilla pod and allow to cool. When cold, churn in an electric ice cream machine, following the manufacturer's instructions. Alternatively, freeze in a freezer-proof container, whisking the mixture every 20 minutes or so until frozen.

To make the maraschino sabayon, put the yolks and 1 tablespoon of water in a large, heatproof glass bowl, placed over a saucepan of boiling water. Beat with a hand whisk or electric beater, until the mixture starts to increase in volume. (The heat will firm the mousse but if you stop beating, you could end up with scrambled eggs.) When the yolks have increased by about three times their original volume, slowly beat in the sugar, which should be accepted readily. This mixture will lose volume but the sugar will stabilise the emulsion.

Beat in the maraschino liqueur and continue to beat until a thick and stable sauce has formed. The consistency should be similar to a fluffy hollandaise. This sauce can be kept covered in a bowl over hot water or in a thermos for the maximum of an hour.

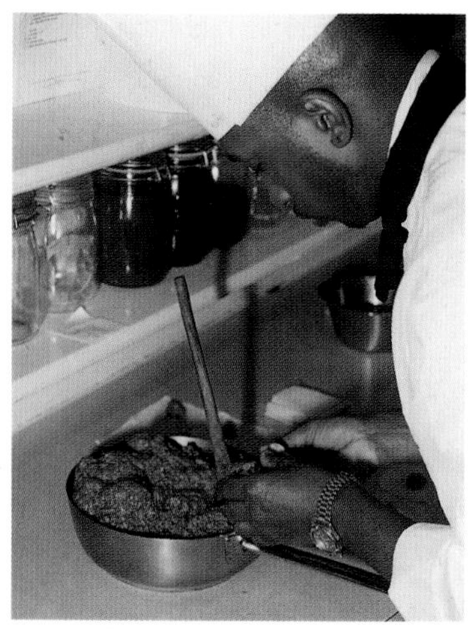

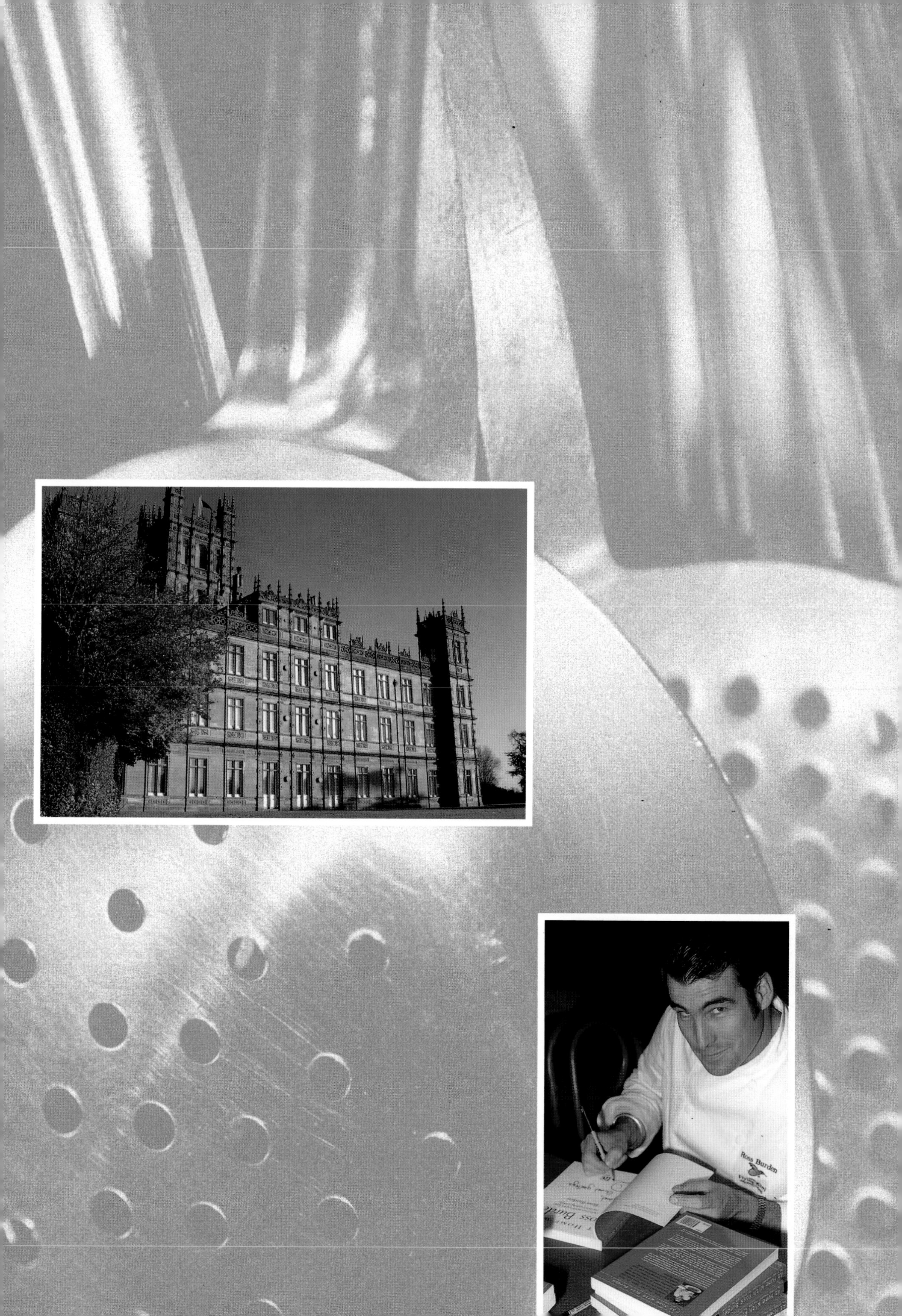
Ross Burden

antonyworrall
thompson

Antony Worrall Thompson is resident chef on the BBC's *Food and Drink* programme and also organises the Young Chef of the Year competition. Winner of numerous culinary awards, Antony acts as a consultant for various restaurants world-wide and writes a regular column for the *Daily Express* and the *Express on Sunday,* as well as his own cookery books. An acclaimed restaurateur, he is passionate about organic food and despite his energetic professional lifestyle he still manages to find time for relaxing pursuits such as art, tennis and swimming.

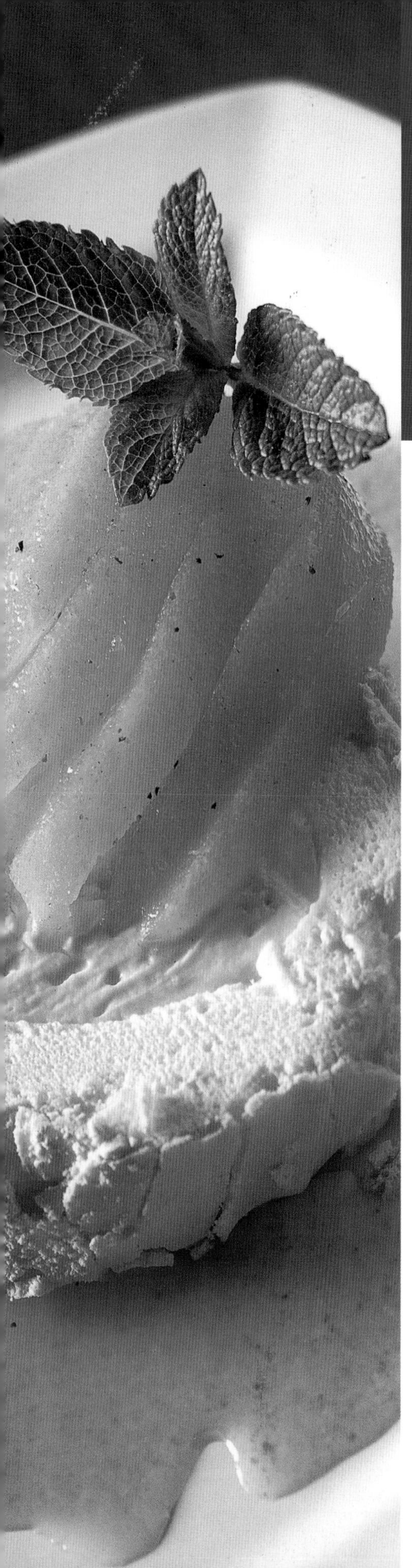

antonyworrall thompson

menu

appetizer or starter

"tapas-style" starter:

shrimp & green onion pancakes

chilli-garlic prawns

vegetable griddle cakes with soured cream & chives

tunisian carrot rolls with apricot dip

skate & sweet spinach salad

truffled burrata with roasted cherry tomatoes

balsamic foie gras

Each of the above can be served on their own as an appetizer or combined to make a stunning "tapas-style" starter which will then serve 10

fish course

monkfish & mussels in spices

main course

prosciutto-wrapped chicken breast
on cep lentils

dessert

pavlova roulade with roasted pear

Bateaux London, on the Thames

wines

white

Villa Maria Sauvignon Blanc, Private Bin, Hawkes Bay 1999, New Zealand

A classic example of a lovely crisp, full-flavoured Sauvignon Blanc wine, which hails from this premium region of New Zealand. Its flavour spectrum of gooseberries, tropical fruits and fresh, citrus acidity makes it an ideal choice for an aperitif or starter dish wine.

Casa La Joya Selection Chardonnay, Colchagua Valley 1998, Chile

Rich and full-bodied with a complex structure, the wine flavours are reminiscent of mangoes and grapefruit, with plenty of upfront tropical fruit aromas. An ideal wine for the monkfish and mussels, the sweetness of the fruit provides an interesting contrast to the spices.

red

Châteauneuf-du-Pape, Domaine de Saint Préfert 1997, France

A traditionally made wine blended from 10 of the permitted grape varieties. Soft with a brambly fruit character, medium acidity, and slight peppery finish, this wine will complement the full-flavoured chicken dish.

dessert

Veuve Clicquot-Ponsardin, White Label, Demi-sec NV, France

A rich, medium-sweet style of Champagne from this traditional Grand Marque house. It has a fruit-driven roundness, with a hint of apples balanced by a ripe acidity. A luxurious partner for the rich pavlova roulade and a great match with the pears.

antonyworrallthompson

"tapas-style" starter:

shrimp & green onion pancakes

makes about 10

1 tablespoon olive oil

bunch of spring onions, finely chopped

25g (1oz) chickpea flour (also called garbanzo or gram flour)

40g (1 1/2oz) plain flour

1/4 teaspoon baking powder

salt and freshly ground black pepper

1 1/2 tablespoons finely chopped fresh parsley

pinch of paprika

100g (4oz) shrimps, shelled and finely chopped

175ml (6fl oz) cold water

oil, for frying

Heat the oil in a saucepan over a low heat. Add the spring onions and cook for 3 minutes, until softened. Leave to cool slightly.

Combine the chickpea flour and plain flour, baking powder, and 1/2 teaspoon each of salt and pepper in a bowl. Add the spring onions, parsley, paprika, shrimps and water, then stir well (the batter should be the consistency of double cream). Leave the batter to rest for 1–2 hours.

In a large heavy-based frying pan, heat the oil (about 5mm/1/4in deep) over a medium heat. For each pancake, pour 2 tablespoons of the batter into the oil and spread it out to make a 5cm (2in) diameter pancake. Fry for 2 minutes on each side, until golden, then drain on kitchen towels. Keep warm and repeat with the remaining batter, then serve immediately with the chilli-garlic prawns below.

pictured on page 63

chilli-garlic prawns

These piquant chilli prawns can be served with the shrimp & green onion pancakes above.

10 large, raw prawns, shells and heads removed, tails left on

juice of 1 lemon

2 large red chillies, deseeded and finely diced

4 cloves garlic, finely diced

salt and freshly ground black pepper

150ml (1/4 pint) extra-virgin olive oil

Make a cut down the back of each prawn, about halfway through the flesh, and remove the dark intestinal vein.

Arrange the prawns on a baking tray and sprinkle with the lemon juice, chillies, garlic, and salt and pepper, then drizzle liberally with the oil. Leave to marinate in the refrigerator for 2 hours to allow the flavours to infuse.

Discard the marinade and cook the prawns in a hot frying pan for about 2 minutes, until pink.

pictured on page 63

vegetable griddle cakes with soured cream & chives

makes about 10

1 large courgette, grated with its skin on

salt and freshly ground black pepper

1 tablespoon extra-virgin olive oil

½ onion, finely chopped

2 cloves garlic, crushed with salt

1 egg

1 tablespoon plain flour

75g (3oz) feta cheese, crumbled

handful of mixed herbs, including fresh flat-leaf parsley, dill and mint, chopped

½ teaspoon chilli flakes

oil, for frying

for the soured cream and chives

150ml (¼ pint) soured cream

2 tablespoons snipped fresh chives

First sprinkle the courgette with salt and leave for 10 minutes, then rinse and drain. Heat the oil in a large frying pan, and fry the onion, courgette and garlic, until just starting to brown.

Beat the egg with the flour in a bowl to make a smooth batter. Add the feta, herbs and chilli flakes and season with salt and pepper. Mix in the warm courgette mixture.

Heat enough oil to coat the base of a heavy-based frying pan. Place a spoonful of the batter in the pan, then cook briefly on each side, until golden.

Combine the soured cream and chives. Season with salt and pepper. Place a spoonful on top of the griddle cakes and serve.

pictured on page 63

antonyworrallthompson

tunisian carrot rolls with apricot dip

makes about 10

5 carrots

1 slice white bread, rubbed into crumbs

3 ready-to-eat dried apricots, finely diced

1 teaspoon sultanas, chopped

2 spring onions, finely chopped

1 tablespoon pine nuts, toasted

2 cloves garlic, finely chopped

½ teaspoon chilli flakes

1 teaspoon grated orange zest

1 egg yolk

handful of parsley

2 tablespoons finely chopped fresh mint

2 tablespoons finely chopped fresh dill

salt and freshly ground black pepper

flour, for coating

oil, for frying

for the apricot dip

4 tablespoons Greek yogurt

1 clove garlic

1 tablespoon lemon juice

4 dried apricots, chopped

First boil the carrots, until tender, then drain well. Mash the carrots, then combine with the remaining ingredients, except the flour and oil. Knead the mixture well – it should be moist and sticky, but if it appears too wet, add more fresh breadcrumbs.

Mould the carrot purée into rolls, using floured hands. Turn each roll in flour, then refrigerate until ready to use.

Heat an oiled frying pan, then fry the carrot rolls briefly, turning occasionally, until golden.

To make the dip, combine the yogurt, garlic, lemon juice and apricots, and serve immediately with the carrot rolls.

"tapas-style" starters shown clockwise, from top left:

vegetable griddle cake with soured cream & chives (recipe page 61), truffled burrata with roasted cherry tomatoes (recipe page 65), tunisian carrot roll with apricot dip, skate and sweet spinach salad (recipe page 64), balsamic foie gras (recipe page 65), and, centre, shrimp & green onion pancake topped with chilli-garlic prawn (recipes page 60)

antonyworrallthompson

skate & sweet spinach salad

serves about 10 as part of tapas

1 skate wing, about 175g (6oz)

1 bay leaf

1 sprig of fresh rosemary

4 black peppercorns

½ lemon, sliced

100g (4oz) spinach leaves, stalks removed, washed thoroughly

1 tablespoon olive oil

½ small red onion, finely chopped

1 clove garlic, crushed

pinch of chilli flakes

15g (½oz) pine nuts

25g (1oz) raisins

½ tablespoon light muscovado sugar

Wash the skate wing and pat dry with kitchen towels. Place the skate in a large saucepan, then add the bay leaf, rosemary, peppercorns, lemon and cover with cold water. Bring to the boil, reduce the heat, and poach for 3–4 minutes, until the fish starts to come away from the bone.

Blanch the spinach in salted water for 3 minutes, until tender, then plunge into cold water and squeeze dry. Finely chop the spinach and set aside.

Heat the oil in a large frying pan. Add the onion and cook for 2 minutes, until translucent. Mix in the garlic, chilli flakes, pine nuts, raisins, sugar and spinach and cook for 1–2 minutes, until combined and warmed through.

With a filleting knife, prise the skate flesh away from the cartilaginous bone on each side. Gently fold the skate into the spinach mixture. Serve cold.

pictured on page 63

truffled burrata with roasted cherry tomatoes

serves about 10 as part of tapas

150g (5oz) ball truffled burrata or buffalo mozzarella, sliced

truffle oil, for drizzling

salt and freshly ground black pepper

1 tablespoon olive oil

1 clove garlic, minced

for the roasted cherry tomatoes

225g (8oz) cherry tomatoes

1 tablespoon sliced shallots

1 tablespoon olive oil

2 tablespoons basil leaves, torn

Drizzle a little truffle oil over the burrata, season with salt and pepper and set aside.

Preheat the oven to 180°C/350°F/ Gas Mark 4. Place the tomatoes and shallots in a baking dish and pour the olive oil over them. Add half the basil, then season to taste. Cook for about 20 minutes, until the tomatoes have softened and are just about to burst.

Remove from the oven and leave the tomatoes and shallots to sit in their juices until ready to serve.

Arrange the truffled burrata on a large plate and drizzle a little more truffle oil over the top. Serve with the roasted tomatoes and shallots and sprinkle with the remaining basil.

pictured on page 63

balsamic foie gras

serves about 10 as part of tapas

salt and freshly ground black pepper

225g (8oz) duck foie gras, sliced into 2.5cm (1in) thick slices

1 tablespoon balsamic vinegar

Lightly season the foie gras on both sides. Heat a large frying pan, until very hot, then briefly sear the slices of foie gras on both sides, remove and set aside. Add the balsamic vinegar and de-glaze the pan by scraping the bottom with a spatula.

Place the foie gras on plates, then pour over the balsamic juices and serve warm.

pictured on page 63

monkfish & mussels in spices

600g (1lb 5oz) monkfish tail, skinned, boned, and cut into 4 even-sized pieces

3/4 teaspoon salt

1 tablespoon lemon juice

pinch of turmeric powder

1/2 teaspoon mustard powder

1/2 teaspoon ground coriander

pinch of ground cumin

pinch of red chilli powder

1/2 teaspoon chopped fresh ginger

1/2 teaspoon chopped fresh garlic

2 1/2 tablespoons oil

1 onion, finely sliced

pinch of fenugreek seeds

1 green chilli, finely chopped

1cm (1/2in) cinnamon stick

3 green cardamom pods

3 cloves

100g (4oz) full-fat yogurt, whipped

1/2 teaspoon sugar

1 tomato, chopped

20 mussels, cleaned

1 1/2 tablespoons sultanas or yellow seedless raisins, soaked in warm water for 20 minutes

Place the monkfish in a shallow dish. Combine 1/2 teaspoon of the salt with the lemon juice and smear the mixture over the fish. Leave for 30 minutes in the refrigerator, then rinse the fish.

Combine the ground spices with the ginger and garlic. Add 50ml (2fl oz) of water to make a paste.

Heat the oil in a large heavy-based saucepan. Add the onions and fry for 12–15 minutes, until softened and lightly browned. Add the fenugreek seeds, chilli, cinnamon, cardamom and cloves. Stir, add the spice paste and cook over a low heat until most of the moisture has evaporated. Sauté the spices for a further 2 minutes, stirring continuously.

Add 120ml (4fl oz) of water to the pan and simmer for 10 minutes, until the mixture has thickened. Reduce the heat to minimum, add the yogurt and stir continuously for 3 minutes. Add the sugar, tomato and salt to taste. Add more water, depending on the consistency of the gravy required, then stir well.

Add the monkfish and mussels and cook for 3 minutes, then turn the fish over. Add the sultanas and cook for 2–3 minutes more, uncovered, until the fish is cooked and the mussels have opened. Discard any mussels that have not opened, and serve.

ρıosciutto-wrapped chicken breast on cep lentils

4 tablespoons olive oil

4 chicken breasts on the bone, skinned, each about 250g (9oz)

8 slices prosciutto

for the cep lentils

1 tablespoon good olive oil

225g (8oz) pancetta or smoked streaky bacon, diced

1 onion, finely chopped

1 carrot, finely chopped

1 stick of celery, finely diced

1 leek, finely chopped

2 bay leaves

1 teaspoon soft thyme leaves

4 cloves garlic, finely chopped

55g (2oz) dried ceps, soaked in 300ml (1/2 pint) boiling water for 30 minutes

225g (8oz) Puy lentils

375ml (13fl oz) gutsy red wine

850ml (1½ pints) chicken or vegetable stock

225g (8oz) chorizo, skinned and cut into 5mm (¼in) slices

55g (2oz) unsalted butter, cubed

4 tablespoons chopped fresh flat-leaf parsley, plus extra to garnish

salt and freshly ground black pepper

First prepare the lentils: heat the olive oil in a heavy-based saucepan. Add the bacon and cook over a medium heat until it is golden and has released its natural fats. Add the onion, carrot, celery, leek, bay leaves, thyme and garlic and cook for 8 minutes.

Drain the ceps and squeeze dry, retaining the soaking liquor. Chop the ceps finely and add to the cooked vegetables. Wash the lentils, add to the pan and stir to combine. Strain the cep soaking liquor through muslin or a fine sieve and add. Take care not to add any grit or murky liquid, so allow the liquor to settle before straining. Add the wine and stock to the lentils, and bring to the boil. Reduce the heat and cook until the lentils are tender, about 35–40 minutes. Some 10 minutes before the lentils are cooked, fold in the chorizo. Just before serving, fold in the butter and parsley. Season to taste.

Meanwhile prepare the chicken breasts. Preheat the oven to 200°C/400°F/ Gas Mark 6. Rub the olive oil over the chicken breasts, then season to taste. Wrap 2 slices of prosciutto around each of the breasts.

Heat a griddle pan and cook the chicken breasts for 5 minutes on each side, or until browned all over. Place the chicken breasts on a baking sheet in the oven and cook for 15 minutes, or until cooked. Season to taste.

Divide the lentils between 4 deep plates, then top with the chicken breasts. Sprinkle with chopped parsley before serving.

pavlova roulade with roasted pear

3 large egg whites

250g (9oz) caster sugar

1 teaspoon vanilla essence

1 teaspoon white wine vinegar

1 teaspoon cornflour

for the mascarpone cream

2 tablespoons caster sugar

3 egg yolks

4 teaspoons Kirsch

225g (8oz) mascarpone

150ml (5fl oz) double cream

roasted pears, to serve (see below)

sprigs of fresh mint, to decorate

Preheat the oven to 160°C/325°F/ Gas Mark 3 and line a 23 x 33cm (9 x 13in) swiss roll tin with baking parchment. Whisk the egg whites until they form stiff peaks. Gradually fold in the sugar, until the mixture becomes thick and glossy. Fold in the vanilla essence, vinegar and cornflour. Using a spatula, spread the meringue in an even layer in the prepared tin and bake for 20–25 minutes, until risen and light golden.

Leave the meringue to cool slightly in the tin for a few minutes, then turn it out onto a sheet of baking paper that has been dusted with icing sugar and leave to cool for 10 minutes.

To make the mascarpone cream, beat the caster sugar with the egg yolks, until it reaches the ribbon stage. Fold in the Kirsch and the mascarpone. Whisk the cream until it forms soft peaks and fold it into the mascarpone mixture.

Spread the mascarpone cream over the meringue and gently roll it up into a roulade using the paper to keep a firm shape. Place the roulade on a tray, cover with plastic film and refrigerate for 3 hours before serving.

Cut the roulade into slices and top each slice with a roasted pear. Drizzle around the pear juices and decorate with a sprig of mint.

roasted pear

4 ripe Conference or Anjou pears, peeled, cored and halved lengthways

2 tablespoons caster sugar

150ml (1/4 pint) sweet white wine

freshly ground black pepper

pinch of grated nutmeg

pinch of ground cinnamon

75g (3oz) unsalted butter, at room temperature

Preheat the oven to 190°C/375°F/ Gas Mark 5. Place the pears, cut-side down in a lightly buttered ovenproof dish. Sprinkle the pears with the sugar and white wine and dust with the spices.

Dot the pears with the butter and bake for about 20 minutes, basting occasionally with the juices, until tender but not mushy. Leave the pears to cool in their juices before slicing lengthways.

kenhom

Ken Hom is the world's unrivalled authority on Chinese cookery. A keen traveller, he regularly tours, advising on Asian cuisine and picking up ideas for recipes. Ken has been a consultant for many prestigious restaurants and hotels all over the world, including the Landmark and the Langham Hilton in London, The Oriental in Bangkok, Silks in San Francisco and London's Imperial City restaurant. He is often invited to prepare banquets for leading figures in business and politics. Ken's books and television series for the BBC have enjoyed phenomenal success and his popularity just keeps rising.

kenhom

menu one

appetizers

crispy chicken with ginger sauce

crispy wontons

fish course

steamed fish with coconut

prawns with green curry

main course

thai barbecue chicken with green bean salad & turmeric rice

dessert

thai-style steamed pumpkin custard

Hopetoun House, Edinburgh

wines

white

Gewürztraminer, Cave Vinicole de Ribeauvillé 1997, France

Gewürztraminer is a distinctively perfumed, exotic, spicy varietal for which Alsace is best known. The pungent lychee bouquet and slightly off-dry palate make a splendid match for many oriental foods, while the spicy character goes well with ginger and chillies.

Oyster Bay, Sauvignon Blanc,
Delegat's Wine Estate 1999, New Zealand

A fine dry white, with the freshness and assertive grassy aroma of well-made Sauvignon Blanc, a crisp acidity and the unique intensity of Marlborough-grown fruit. Not only is this grape variety particularly good with most light fish dishes, but its juicy, herby, fruity character enlivens the palate after the rich coconut and green curry flavours.

red

Bel Arbor Merlot 1997, California

A concentrated wine packed with a soft plummy varietal flavour. The wine is blended with a touch of Carignan and matured in American oak. This gives it a supple, spicy, rounded finish, perfect with the barbecue sauce. Merlot also has a secret: it goes extremely well with coriander, a major element of Thai cuisine, enhancing and sweetening the flavour.

dessert

Côteaux du Layon, Moulin Touchais, Vignobles Touchais
1984, France

Rich and luscious, but with a wonderful acidity which prevents any cloying on the palate. A first-class example of sweet, Loire, Chenin Blanc from a top producer. It has a delicate flavour and will not overwhelm the delicate Thai flavours. The cleansing acidity on the finish will complement the rich pumpkin custard, ready for the next mouthful.

kenhom

crispy chicken with ginger sauce

This dish makes an appealing appetizer or a snack to have with drinks. The light, but rich-tasting sauce enhances the flavour of the breaded chicken.

5½–6½ tablespoons groundnut (peanut) oil

3 tablespoons finely chopped fresh ginger

1½ tablespoons lime juice

1 tablespoon sugar

2 tablespoons honey

2 tablespoons fish sauce or light soy sauce

250ml (8fl oz) homemade chicken stock or store-bought fresh stock

1 tablespoon cornflour mixed with 2 tablespoons water

450g (1lb) boneless chicken breasts, skinned, about 4 pieces

1½ teaspoons salt

½ teaspoon freshly ground 5-spice or black pepper

plain flour, for dusting

1 egg, beaten

225g (8oz) dried breadcrumbs

First make the ginger sauce: heat a wok or frying pan until it is hot and add 1½ tablespoons of the oil. When the oil is slightly smoking, add the ginger and stir-fry for 2 minutes, until golden brown. Add the lime juice, sugar, honey, fish sauce and stock and simmer for 1 minute. Drizzle in the cornflour and water mixture, stirring continuously until the sauce has thickened slightly. Remove from the heat and allow to cool. Set aside.

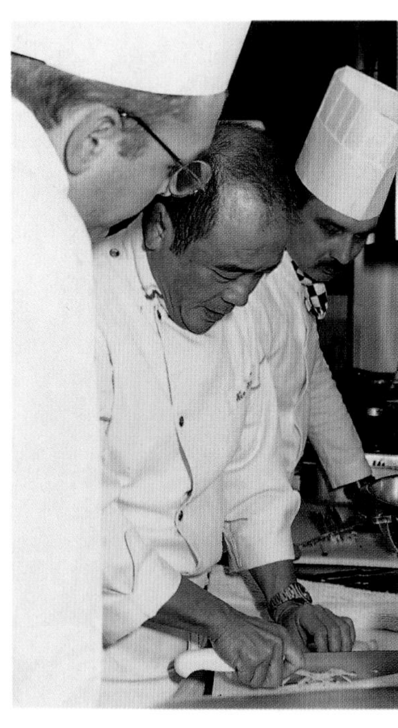

Place each chicken breast between two pieces of cling film. With a large wooden mallet or empty bottle, pound the chicken until it is flat and thin, about 5mm (¼in) thick.

Sprinkle the salt and pepper evenly over the chicken, then dust with flour, shaking off any excess. Dip the chicken in the beaten egg and finally in the breadcrumbs.

Heat a wok or large frying pan and add 2 tablespoons of the remaining oil. Turn the heat down to moderate and slowly pan-fry the chicken on one side for 5 minutes, until it is golden brown, then turn over and brown the other side. Add more oil as necessary. Remove the chicken, cut it into bite-sized pieces and serve with the ginger sauce.

crispy wontons

serves 6

100g (4oz) raw prawns, peeled

350g (12oz) minced pork

2 teaspoons salt

1 teaspoon freshly ground black pepper

2 tablespoons finely chopped garlic

3 tablespoons finely chopped spring onions

2 tablespoons fish sauce or light soy sauce

1 teaspoon sugar

3 tablespoons finely chopped fresh coriander

1 egg, lightly beaten

225g (8oz) wonton wrappers

400ml (14fl oz) groundnut (peanut) oil, for deep frying

for the spicy dipping sauce (*nam prik pla*)

2–3 small fresh red Thai chillies, seeded and sliced

1 tablespoon sugar

3 tablespoons fish sauce or light soy sauce

3 tablespoons lime juice

2 teaspoons water

Using a small, sharp knife, make a cut down the back of each prawn and remove the fine intestinal cord. Wash the prawns in cold water, rinse and pat dry with kitchen paper, then coarsely chop.

Put the prawns and pork in a large bowl, add the salt and pepper and mix well, either kneading with your hands or stirring with a wooden spoon. Add the rest of the filling ingredients, down to and including the egg, and stir well. Cover the bowl with cling film and chill for about 20 minutes.

To make the dipping sauce, combine the chillies, sugar, fish sauce, lime juice and water in a bowl. Mix well and set aside while you prepare the wontons.

To stuff the wontons, put 1 tablespoon of the prawn and pork filling in the centre of a wonton wrapper. Dampen the edges with a little water and bring up the sides around the filling. Pinch the edges together at the top to seal the wonton parcel. Repeat until you have used up all the wonton wrappers and filling.

Heat the oil in a deep-fat fryer or a large wok until it is hot. Deep-fry the wontons, a few at a time, for 3 minutes, or until golden and crispy. Drain the wontons well on kitchen paper. Serve immediately with the dipping sauce.

steamed fish with coconut

This Thai-inspired dish uses coconut milk, in combination with lemongrass and kaffir lime leaves, to make a fragrant, silky sauce that highlights the subtle flavour of the fish.

2 stalks fresh lemongrass

400ml (14fl oz) can coconut milk

2 tablespoons coarsely chopped fresh galangal root or ginger

6 fresh kaffir lime leaves or 2 tablespoons lime zest

450g (1lb) firm white fish fillets, such as cod, sole or turbot

3 tablespoons finely sliced shallots

3 tablespoons fish sauce or light soy sauce

2 tablespoons lime juice

1 tablespoon sugar

2 teaspoons chilli oil

handful of fresh coriander leaves, to garnish

Remove the outer layers of the lemongrass and crush the tender, whitish centre with the flat of a knife, then cut into 7.5cm (3in) pieces. In a large saucepan, combine the lemongrass, coconut milk, galangal and lime leaves. Cover and simmer for 1 hour. Strain and discard the solids.

Fill a steamer or put a rack into a wok or deep pan, and pour in 5cm (2in) of water. Bring the water to the boil over a high heat.

Pat the fish fillets dry with kitchen paper. Put the fish on a deep, heatproof plate and pour the coconut mixture over the top. Add the shallots, fish sauce, lime juice and sugar. Put the plate into the steamer or onto the rack. Cover the pan tightly and gently steam the fish until it is just cooked and tender. Flat fish will take about 5 minutes to cook, while thicker fish or fillets, such as sea bass, will take 8–12 minutes.

Remove the fish from the steamer. Divide the fish between 4 plates and spoon around the sauce. Drizzle with chilli oil and garnish with the coriander, then serve.

kenhom

prawns with green curry

450g (1lb) raw prawns, peeled

1 1/2 tablespoons groundnut (peanut) oil

3 tablespoons coarsely chopped garlic

2 tablespoons finely sliced shallots

2 teaspoons cumin seeds

1 teaspoon shrimp paste

2 tablespoons Thai green curry paste

400ml (14fl oz) can coconut milk

1 tablespoon fish sauce or light soy sauce

2 teaspoons sugar

small handful of fresh basil leaves, shredded

4 fresh kaffir lime leaves or 1 tablespoon lime zest

handful of fresh coriander leaves

Using a small, sharp knife, make a cut down the back of each prawn and remove the fine intestinal cord. Wash the prawns in cold water and pat them dry with kitchen paper.

Heat a wok or large frying pan until it is very hot. Add the oil, garlic, shallots and cumin seeds and stir-fry for 5 minutes or until well toasted. Add the shrimp paste and curry paste and stir-fry for 2 minutes. Add the coconut milk, fish sauce, sugar, basil leaves, lime leaves and the prawns. Reduce the heat and simmer for 5 minutes, stirring from time to time.

When the prawns are cooked, add the coriander leaves and give the sauce a good stir, then serve accompanied by rice.

thai barbecue chicken

Barbecued or grilled food, otherwise known as "sate" or "satay", plays a prominent role in Thai cooking. The secret of excellence is in the marinating and the marinade sauce, which must be left for some time to impart its flavours. I recommend marinating food overnight for best results.

Serve this with the green bean salad and turmeric rice on page 85.

900g (2lb) chicken thighs, on the bone

for the marinade

2 tablespoons fish sauce or light soy sauce

3 tablespoons coarsely chopped garlic

3 tablespoons finely chopped fresh coriander

2 small fresh red or green Thai chillies, deseeded and chopped

2 teaspoons sugar

1 tablespoon Shaoxing rice wine or dry sherry

1 teaspoon turmeric

2 teaspoons Thai red curry paste

1 teaspoon salt

1/2 teaspoon freshly ground black pepper

4 tablespoons canned coconut milk

Pat the chicken thighs dry with kitchen paper and place in a large bowl. In a blender or food processor, blend the ingredients for the marinade to make a thick paste. Spoon the marinade over the chicken and turn until coated. Cover with cling film and refrigerate overnight.

When you are ready to barbecue or grill the chicken, remove it from the refrigerator and leave at room temperature for 40 minutes.

Make a charcoal fire in the barbecue or preheat the oven grill to high. When the charcoal is ash white or the oven grill is very hot, grill the chicken thighs for about 10 minutes on each side or until cooked. Baste the chicken regularly with the marinade during cooking.

Place the chicken on a warm platter and serve immediately, or allow to cool and serve at room temperature.

kenhom

green bean salad

serves 2–4

450g (1lb) winged beans or runner beans, or French beans, trimmed and sliced if long, otherwise left whole

2 small fresh red or green Thai chillies, deseeded and chopped

1 teaspoon sugar

2 tablespoons lime juice

2 tablespoons light soy sauce

200ml (7fl oz) canned coconut milk

3 tablespoons finely sliced shallots

for the garnish

3 tablespoons roasted peanuts, crushed

2 tablespoons desiccated coconut, roasted for 3 minutes in a hot oven

Blanch the beans in salted boiling water for 3 minutes. Drain and plunge them immediately in cold water, then drain thoroughly and set aside.

Combine the chillies, sugar, lime juice, soy sauce and coconut milk in a bowl and mix well. Toss the blanched beans and shallots into the chilli mixture. Garnish with peanuts and roasted desiccated coconut and serve.

turmeric rice

serves 4–6

long-grain white rice, measured to the 400ml (14fl oz) level in a measuring jug

3 tablespoons groundnut (peanut) oil

2 tablespoons coarsely chopped garlic

175g (6oz) onion, finely chopped

100g (4oz) fresh button mushrooms, sliced

2 teaspoons turmeric powder

½ teaspoon freshly ground black pepper

1 teaspoon sugar

1 tablespoon Madras curry powder

1 tablespoon fish sauce or light soy sauce

3 tablespoons finely chopped spring onions, to garnish

Cook the rice at least 2 hours ahead of serving or the night before. Allow to cool thoroughly and store in the refrigerator.

Heat a wok or large frying pan over a high heat until it is hot. Add the oil and when it is slightly smoking, add the garlic and onion and stir-fry for 2 minutes. Add the mushrooms and cook for 2 minutes more. Add the rice and stir-fry for 3 minutes. Stir in the turmeric, pepper, sugar and curry powder and stir-fry for 2 minutes, then add the fish sauce and stir-fry for a further minute.

Place on a platter, garnish with the spring onions. Serve hot, or cold as a rice salad.

thai-style steamed pumpkin custard

In Thailand, this custard is steamed inside a small pumpkin. However, here it is served in ramekins. It can be eaten hot or cold.

serves 6

450g (1lb) cooked pumpkin or squash

5 eggs, beaten

175g (6oz) sugar

½ teaspoon salt

400ml (14fl oz) can coconut milk

Purée the cooked pumpkin or squash in a food processor or blender. Add the eggs, sugar, salt and coconut milk and blend until puréed. Pour the mixture into ramekins or small dishes.

Place a rack in a wok or deep pan or alternatively use a steamer. Fill the wok or pan with 5cm (2in) of water. Bring the water to the boil, then carefully place the ramekins or dishes on the rack or in the steamer. Turn the heat to low and cover tightly.

Steam gently for 20 minutes, or until the custard has set. Remove and serve, or allow the custards to cool before serving.

kenhom

menu two

appetizers

thai meatballs

vietnamese-style spring rolls

soup course

classic wonton soup

fish course

singapore curry crab

main course

thai chicken with hong kong-style broccoli & baby corn

dessert

chocolate cake with candied ginger

The Honourable Society of Kings Inns, Dublin

wines

white

Pinot Blanc, Les Ecumes, Cave Vinicole de Ribeauvillé 1998, France

This close relative of the Chardonnay grape produces a delicately flavoured wine with a refreshing appley palate and citrus finish. Its light style complements the Thai meatballs and Vietnamese spring rolls.

Pinot Grigio del Veneto, Corta Vigna 1998, Italy

Soup, particularly delicately flavoured examples such as this light wonton soup, match best with light, crisp dry whites, without too strong flavours. This Pinot Grigio from north-east Italy has just enough floral fruit character to complement, without overpowering, the dish.

Viognier, Vin de Pays d'Oc, Jean d'Alibert 1998, France

Ripe and rich, with aromas of peaches and apricots – both classic Viognier flavour characteristics – this may not seem the first choice to match with a spicy crab curry. However, it has a lovely mouthfilling palate, an acidity that balances the richness of the dish.

red

Samur Rouge, Domaine des Salaises, Andre Benoist 1997, France

A light-bodied Loire red is an ideal wine for many chicken dishes, providing a little tannin that does not overpower other aspects of the dish, and a bright, berry fruit palate.

dessert

Seppelt Show Sparkling Shiraz 1986, Australia

Chocolate is one of the most difficult foods with which to partner wine. However, this red, sparkling wine is smooth and mellow with great richness and complexity and a spicy, almost chocolatey palate.

kenhom

thai meatballs

I first tasted this dish in Bangkok, from one of the many street vendors there. The meatballs have a delicate, light texture and a delicious blend of spices which complement the minced pork and beef.

100g (4oz) minced beef

100g (4oz) minced pork

2 egg whites

2 tablespoons very cold water

1 teaspoon salt

½ teaspoon freshly ground black pepper

2 tablespoons finely chopped garlic

3 tablespoons finely chopped fresh coriander

3 tablespoons finely chopped spring onions

2 teaspoons Thai fish sauce

2 teaspoons sugar

plain flour, for dusting

450ml (¾ pint) groundnut (peanut) oil

Mix the beef and pork in a food processor for a few seconds. Slowly add the egg whites and cold water and mix for a few seconds until they have combined with the meat. Then add the rest of the ingredients, except the flour and oil, and mix for about a minute until the meat mixture has become a light paste.

Using your hands, form the mixture into 4cm (1½in) balls, about the size of a golf ball. (This recipe makes about 10 balls.) Dust them evenly with the flour, shaking off any excess. Handle them gently – the meatballs will be quite fragile and soft.

Heat a wok or large frying-pan over a high heat until it is hot. Add the oil and, when it is very hot and slightly smoking, gently drop in as many meatballs as will fit easily in one layer. Carefully fry them for about 4 minutes, until the meatballs are crispy and browned. (You may have to do this in several batches.)

Remove the meatballs with a slotted spoon and drain on kitchen paper. Serve immediately.

vietnamese-style spring rolls

makes about 25

5 tablespoons plain flour

5 tablespoons water

1 packet rice paper wrappers

450ml (¾ pint) oil, preferably groundnut (peanut)

225g (8oz) iceberg lettuce

sprigs of fresh herbs such as basil, mint or coriander, or a combination of all three

for the filling

25g (1oz) beanthread (transparent) noodles

15g (½oz) Chinese dried wood ear mushrooms

1 tablespoon groundnut (peanut) oil

1 small onion, finely chopped

2 tablespoons coarsely chopped garlic

2 tablespoons finely chopped spring onions

2 tablespoons finely chopped shallots

225g (8oz) minced pork

½ teaspoon freshly ground black pepper

1½ teaspoons salt

175g (6oz) cooked fresh crabmeat

for the dipping sauce

4 tablespoons Thai fish sauce

1 teaspoon dried chilli powder or flakes

1 tablespoon finely chopped garlic

1 tablespoon lime juice

4 tablespoons water

1 tablespoon sugar

First make the dipping sauce: combine the ingredients in a blender, mixing them thoroughly. Allow the mixture to sit for at least 10 minutes before using.

To make the filling, soak the noodles in a large bowl of warm water for 15 minutes. When soft, drain and discard the water. Cut the noodles into 7.5cm (3in) lengths using scissors or a knife.

Soak the wood ear mushrooms in warm water for about 20 minutes, until soft. Rinse well in cold water and squeeze to remove any excess liquid. Remove any hard stems and shred the caps finely.

Heat the wok or large frying-pan over a high heat until it is hot. Add the oil, and when it is very hot and slightly smoking, add the onion, garlic, spring onions and shallots and stir-fry for 3 minutes. Add the pork, pepper and salt and continue to stir-fry for 5 minutes. Drain the pork mixture in a colander and allow to cool.

When the pork mixture is cool, place it in a large bowl with the beanthread noodles, wood ears and cooked crabmeat.

In a small bowl, mix the flour and water into a paste. When you are ready to make the spring rolls, fill a large bowl with warm water. Dip one of the rice paper rounds into the water and allow it to soften. Remove and drain on a linen tea towel. Put about 2 tablespoons of the filling on a softened rice paper wrapper and then roll it up tightly. Seal the ends with a little of the flour paste mixture. You should have a roll about 7.5cm (3in) in length. Repeat this until you have used up the wrappers and filling.

Heat the oil in a deep-fat fryer or a large pan until it is hot. Deep-fry the spring rolls until they are golden brown. They have a tendency to stick to each other at the beginning of the frying, so only cook a few at a time. Do not attempt to break them apart should they stick together. You can do this after they have been removed from the oil. Drain them on kitchen paper.

Serve the spring rolls at once with the lettuce leaves, herb sprigs and the dipping sauce.

classic wonton soup

At their best, wontons are filled with savoury meats, vegetables and seasonings. Gently poached and floating in a rich, clear chicken stock, they make a dish that is at once exotic and familiar. The light, sheer dough that serves as a wrapper can be easily purchased in Chinese grocers and sometimes in large supermarkets.

1 packet wonton wrappers

1 litre (1¾ pints) chicken stock

1 tablespoon light soy sauce

1 teaspoon toasted sesame oil

3 tablespoons chopped spring onions, to garnish

2 tablespoons fresh coriander leaves, to garnish

for the wonton filling

225g (8oz) raw prawns, peeled, deveined and chopped

225g (8oz) fatty minced pork

175g (6oz) fresh water chestnuts, peeled and chopped, or 75g (3oz) canned water chestnuts

1 teaspoon salt

½ teaspoon freshly ground black pepper

3 tablespoons finely chopped spring onions

1 tablespoon finely chopped fresh ginger

1 tablespoon light soy sauce

1 teaspoon dark soy sauce

2 teaspoons Shaoxing rice wine or dry sherry

1 teaspoon sugar

2 teaspoons toasted sesame oil

1 egg white, lightly beaten

Combine the wonton filling ingredients in a large bowl and mix well. Allow to marinate for about 20 minutes.

Place about 1 tablespoon of the filling in the centre of a wonton wrapper. Dampen the edges of the wrapper with water and bring the sides of the dough up around the filling. Pinch the edges together at the top to seal; it will look like a small sack. Continue to fill all the wonton wrappers.

When the wontons have been made, bring the stock to a simmer, stirring in the soy sauce and sesame oil.

In another pot, bring salted water to the boil and poach the wontons for 1 minute. Remove them with a strainer and put them into the simmering stock. Continue to simmer the wontons for 2 minutes.

Ladle the wontons and soup into a large soup tureen or individual bowls. Garnish with the spring onions and coriander leaves and serve at once.

kenhom

singapore curry crab

I have adapted this classic dish, which combines the flavours of China and India, to create my own blend of spices. Serve it with plain rice and a vegetable dish for a complete meal. Remember, it is important to buy the freshest crab available, preferably live.

1.4kg (3lb) live or freshly cooked whole crab

2 stalks fresh lemongrass, cut into 5cm (2in) pieces

2 tablespoons groundnut (peanut) oil

8 cloves garlic, thinly sliced

2 tablespoons finely shredded fresh root ginger

4 tablespoons thinly sliced small onions or shallots

3 tablespoons finely shredded spring onions

3 tablespoons Madras curry paste

400ml (14fl oz) can coconut milk

1 teaspoon salt

2 teaspoons sugar

To cook a live crab, bring a large saucepan of water to the boil, drop in the crab and boil until there is no movement; this will take about 2 minutes. Remove the crab and drain thoroughly.

Remove the tail-flap, push the body with legs still attached away from the shell and remove the stomach sac and feathery gills from the crab. Using a heavy knife or cleaver, cut the crab, shell included, into large pieces.

With the flat side of a large knife or cleaver, smash the lemongrass pieces to release their oils.

Heat a wok or large frying pan over a high heat until it is hot. Add the oil and, when it is very hot and slightly smoking, add the lemongrass pieces, garlic, ginger and onions or shallots and stir-fry for 1 minute. Add the spring onions and crab pieces and stir-fry for 2 minutes.

Add the remaining ingredients and continue to stir-fry the mixture over a high heat for about 2 minutes. Turn the heat to low, cover, and simmer for 10 minutes.

Turn the curry on to a large, warm serving platter and serve.

thai chicken

In this Thai-inspired dish, I have taken elements of Thai flavourings such as lemongrass, garlic and fresh chillies, and have combined them to create my own delicious chicken dish. A good accompaniment is the hong kong-style broccoli & baby corn dish on page 98.

450g (1lb) skinless, boneless chicken thighs or 900g (2lb) chicken thighs with bone

1 stalk fresh lemongrass, tough outer layers removed and cut into 5cm (2in) pieces

1 tablespoon groundnut (peanut) oil

1 onion, thinly sliced

2 teaspoons salt

2 tablespoons coarsely chopped garlic

2 teaspoons finely chopped lime zest

3 fresh red or green chillies, deseeded and sliced into rounds

2 teaspoons sugar

large handful of fresh basil leaves

for the marinade

2 teaspoons light soy sauce

2 teaspoons Shaoxing rice wine or dry sherry

1 teaspoon sesame oil

2 teaspoons cornflour

Mix together the ingredients for the marinade in a bowl.

If you are using chicken thighs on the bone, remove the skin and the bones or have your butcher do it for you. Cut the chicken into 2.5cm (1in) chunks and put it in a large bowl. Pour the marinade over the chicken and stir to coat the meat. Leave to marinate for 20 minutes.

Smash the pieces of lemongrass with the flat of a knife or cleaver.

Heat a wok or large frying-pan until it is very hot. Add the oil, then the chicken and stir-fry for 5 minutes, until the chicken has browned. Remove the chicken and drain off the oil. Return the drained chicken to the wok and add the rest of the ingredients, except the basil leaves.

Cook for a further 8–10 minutes, stirring from time to time, until the chicken has cooked. Add the basil leaves and give the mixture a good stir. Spoon on to a warm platter or 4 individual plates and serve at once.

Top, hong kong-style broccoli and baby corn (recipe page 98); and below, thai chicken

kenhom

hong kong-style broccoli & baby corn

This is a very easy dish to prepare in a wok, and to serve as a side dish. If you use the dark soy sauce instead of the oyster sauce, it would make this dish a good one for vegetarians.

450g (1lb) broccoli, cut into small florets, stems peeled and sliced

225g (8oz) baby corn

50g (2oz) Chinese black mushrooms, soaked in warm water for 20 minutes

1½ tablespoons groundnut (peanut) oil

1 teaspoon salt

½ teaspoon freshly ground black pepper

1 teaspoon sugar

1 tablespoon Shaoxing rice wine or dry sherry

1 tablespoon light soy sauce

3 tablespoons oyster sauce or dark soy sauce

2 teaspoons sesame oil

Blanch the broccoli and baby corn in a large pan of boiling water for 3 minutes, then immerse them in cold water. Drain thoroughly.

Drain the mushrooms and squeeze to remove any excess liquid. Remove and discard the stems and finely shred the caps into thin strips.

Heat a wok or large frying pan over a high heat until it is hot. Add the oil and, when it is very hot and slightly smoking, add the broccoli, corn and mushrooms and stir-fry for 3 minutes.

Add the salt, pepper, sugar, Shaoxing rice wine or dry sherry, soy sauce and oyster sauce or dark soy sauce and continue to stir-fry over a moderate to high heat for 2 minutes, until the vegetables are thoroughly heated through and slightly softened.

Add the sesame oil and continue to stir-fry for 30 seconds. Transfer to a warm platter or 4 individual plates and serve at once.

chocolate cake with candied ginger

Chocolate is rarely found on Asian menus or in homes. However, now that Asians have tasted this western flavour, it has become very popular. In this classic chocolate cake, I have combined it with candied ginger to give an eastern zest to the western dessert.

serves 6–8

350g (12oz) finest quality dark chocolate, broken into pieces

150g (5oz) unsalted butter

135g (4¾oz) granulated sugar

50g (2oz) candied ginger, finely chopped

4 egg yolks

40g (1½oz) plain flour, sifted

6 egg whites

icing sugar, sifted, for dusting

Preheat the oven to 180°C/350°F/Gas mark 4. Combine the chocolate, butter, sugar and ginger in a heatproof bowl, placed over a large pan of boiling water. Melt the mixture over a moderate heat, stirring constantly, until the ingredients have combined. Leave the mixture to cool.

Whisk in the egg yolks and then the flour. Mix thoroughly.

Whisk the egg whites until they form firm peaks. Add a third of the egg whites to the chocolate mixture, mix vigorously, then fold in the remaining egg whites.

Butter a 20–23cm (8–9in) cake tin. Pour in the cake mixture and bake for 35–40 minutes, until firm. Allow the cake to cool completely. Turn the cake onto a platter, dust with icing sugar and serve.

garyrhodes

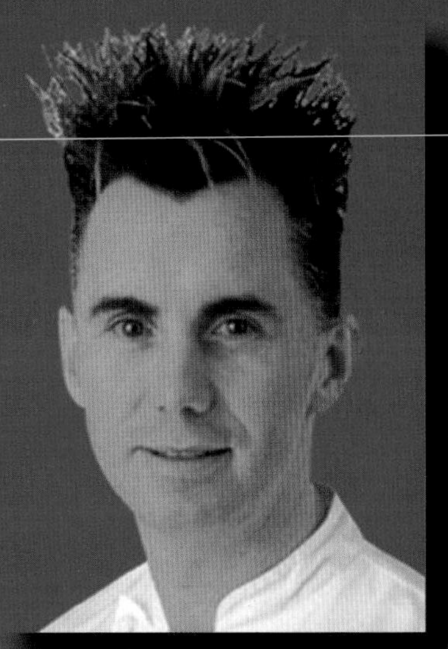

Gary Rhodes' early career was spent at the Amsterdam Hilton, the Reform Club and the Capital Hotel in London followed by The Castle Hotel in Taunton. At The Castle Hotel, with Kit Chapman's encouragement, Gary developed a repertoire of traditional favourites often centred on less fashionable cuts of meats, braised and stewed to extract maximum flavour. After appearing on *Hot Chefs* he was offered his own television series – *Rhodes Around Britain,* and produced a book to accompany the series. Gary's working relationship with Sodexho commenced with the opening of City Rhodes, quickly followed by Rhodes in the Square, and Rhodes & Co. Restaurants in Manchester and Edinburgh. The many accolades Gary has earned include Michelin stars in three of his restaurants and a CATEY award in 1996 for his contribution to the British Food Industry. Continued television and best-selling cookery books for the BBC have confirmed Gary Rhodes as a household name.

garyrhodes

menu

fish course

ballotine of salmon on caramelised shallots, capers & black olives with a saffron water dressing

main course

roasted tournedos of lamb on seared artichoke filled with a cèpe duxelle

dessert

iced vanilla parfait with roasted nutmeg apples

Sodexho, as Founder Members of The Duke of Edinburgh's Award Scheme, had a unique opportunity to use the special skills of Gary Rhodes to prepare a Master Class Gala Dinner at St James's Palace for other Founder and Charter For Business Members in the presence of His Royal Highness The Duke of Edinburgh.

St James's Palace, London

wines

white

Pouilly-Fuissé, Louis Jadot 1997, France

A full-flavoured dry white wine made from the Chardonnay grape, which has been fermented and aged in oak barrels to give greater complexity and weight. Chardonnay and salmon is a great match, both have a similar concentration of flavours, and the lemony aspect of the wine is perfect with the oily fish.

red

The Menzies, Cabernet Sauvignon, Yalumba 1996, Australia

A rich, velvety red, with bold fruit flavours and named in honour of an Australian Prime Minister, Sir Robert Menzies, who proclaimed it his favourite wine. This is another example of how important it is to match wine with food: the lamb, ceps and artichokes are all full flavoured enough not to be overwhelmed by the wine.

dessert

Côteaux du Layon, Moulin Touchais, Vignobles Touchais 1984, France

A rich, luscious wine with a ripe honeyed character and a long lingering finish from one of the top producers in the Loire Valley. The relatively high acidity of the wine and its delicate nature (being from the northerly upper Loire), make it a refreshing match for the light, creamy parfait.

garyrhodes

ballotine of salmon on caramelised shallots, capers & black olives with a saffron water dressing

serves 8

3.6–4.2kg/8–9lb salmon (2 sides), skinned, filleted, cleaned and pin bones removed

a large knob of butter, melted

100–150g (4–5oz) smoked salmon

5 tablespoons olive oil

24 large shallots, cut into 1cm (1/2in) dice

1 teaspoon soft brown sugar (optional)

salt and freshly ground black pepper

2 large lemons, peeled, segmented and sliced

24–28 black olives, quartered

2 tablespoons capers

2 tablespoons chopped fresh chives

for the cure

100g (4oz) sea salt

100g (4oz) sugar

zest of 1 lemon

1 measure brandy

for the saffron water dressing

small pinch of saffron strands

120ml (4fl oz) water

120ml (4fl oz) olive oil

freshly squeezed lemon juice

First cure the salmon: combine the ingredients for the cure and rub into the flesh of the salmon. Chill for 12 hours, then rinse.

Lay the sides of salmon, skinned side up, on top of each other, head to tail, on a double sheet of cling film, roll very tightly to form a cylinder shape, secure, then chill. When chilled, poach the salmon in water for 12 minutes, until just cooked, then remove from the heat and set aside for another 10–12 minutes. Once cold and set, remove the salmon from the cling film and brush lightly with the melted butter, then wrap in slices of smoked salmon, re-wrap in cling film and leave to chill.

Heat a tablespoon of the oil, add the shallots and sauté over a low heat. Add the sugar, if using, and cook for 8 minutes, until they are a deep golden colour and have caramelised. Season with salt and pepper, then add the rest of the oil to the pan.

Add the sliced lemons, olives, capers and chives and heat gently. Spoon the mixture into 8 x 7.5cm (3 inch) round moulds, press down firmly and set aside.

To make the saffron water dressing, combine the saffron strands and the water in a pan and bring to the boil. Boil briefly to allow the saffron to infuse, then whisk in the olive oil and lemon juice.

To serve, remove the ring moulds and top with a slice of the salmon ballotine. Drizzle around the saffron water dressing.

roast tournedos of lamb on sea... artichoke filled with a cèpe duxelle

serves 8

Tournedos is a description usually used for beef fillet steaks. Lamb does not provide the same size of fillet but this recipe is achieved using a leg of lamb. The technique provides the beef fillet finish – a very tender meat.

8 globe artichokes

juice of 1 lemon

1 leg of lamb, boned and fat removed, about 1.5kg (3½lb)

salt and freshly ground black pepper

pinch of ground cumin

175g (6oz) pig's caul fat (optional)

25g (1oz) butter, plus extra for greasing

8 cèpes, left whole

for the artichoke stock

4 very ripe tomatoes, roughly chopped

juice of 1 lemon

300ml (½ pint) water

1 teaspoon coriander seeds

1 bay leaf

for the sauce

½ bottle red wine

600ml (1 pint) veal or beef jus/gravy

for the cèpe duxelle

225g (8oz) each of chestnut, button and cèpe mushrooms, coarsely chopped

25g (1oz) butter

First make the stock: place all the ingredients in a pan and bring to a simmer. The stock will help to retain the colour of the artichokes and enhance their flavour.

To prepare the artichokes, remove the stalks and then cut around the base, removing the outer leaves. Cut across the base, about 2–3mm (⅛in) from the bottom. The centre of the base should still be intact. Rub the artichokes with lemon juice.

Place the artichoke bottoms and the remaining lemon juice in the stock and simmer for 25 minutes, until tender. Cool, then remove the "thistley" centre.

Separate the boned leg of lamb into individual muscles by pulling apart the membranes which hold them together. Remove the sinews until you have small pieces of lean meat. (It is important that the sinews are totally removed, since they affect the tenderness of the meat.) Cut the meat into 10cm (4in) long x 1cm (½in) strips or fillets.

Mince or process the trimmings or leftover meat – make sure you have about 100g (4oz). Season with salt and pepper and the ground cumin. This "farce" is used to hold the meat together once the tournedos have been assembled.

Rinse the pig's caul, if using, in cold water to loosen the lacy texture, and place on a sheet of buttered foil. If not using the caul, replace with a buttered sheet of parchment paper. Lay the lamb fillets horizontally on the caul. Lay them side by side, which will give you a line of meat, approximately 7.5–10cm (3–4in) wide x 30cm (12in) long. Spread the minced lamb thinly over the top and then roll or shape into a cylinder. Wrap tightly in the caul/paper and buttered foil and then wrap in extra foil, twisting at either end until firm. Leave in the refrigerator for 1–2 hours.

Preheat the oven to 200°C/400°F/

Gas Mark 6. Cut the cylinder into 8 tournedos. Remove the foil and tie each portion with two pieces of string to retain their shape.

To cook the lamb, season with salt and pepper and pan-fry carefully in the butter until coloured top and bottom. Transfer to a roasting tin and finish in the oven for 8–10 minutes. The lamb should still be pink in the centre. Remove the lamb from the oven and leave to rest and tenderise for about 4–5 minutes. If using parchment paper, simply remove and, for extra "roasted" colour, pan-fry around the sides.

To make the sauce, boil the wine vigorously until reduced by three-quarters and add the jus. Cook for 5–10 minutes, then pass through a sieve.

To make the cèpe duxelle, sauté all the chopped mushrooms in butter until they are tender. Season with salt and pepper and set aside.

Sauté the artichoke bottoms face down in butter, until lightly coloured and warmed through. Meanwhile, preheat the grill to high. Brush the whole cèpes with melted butter and grill until tender.

To serve, fill the hollowed cavities of the artichokes with the chopped mushroom mixture and place on 8 plates. Sit the tournedos of lamb on top and, finally, top with a grilled cèpe cap and spoon the sauce over and around the finished dish.

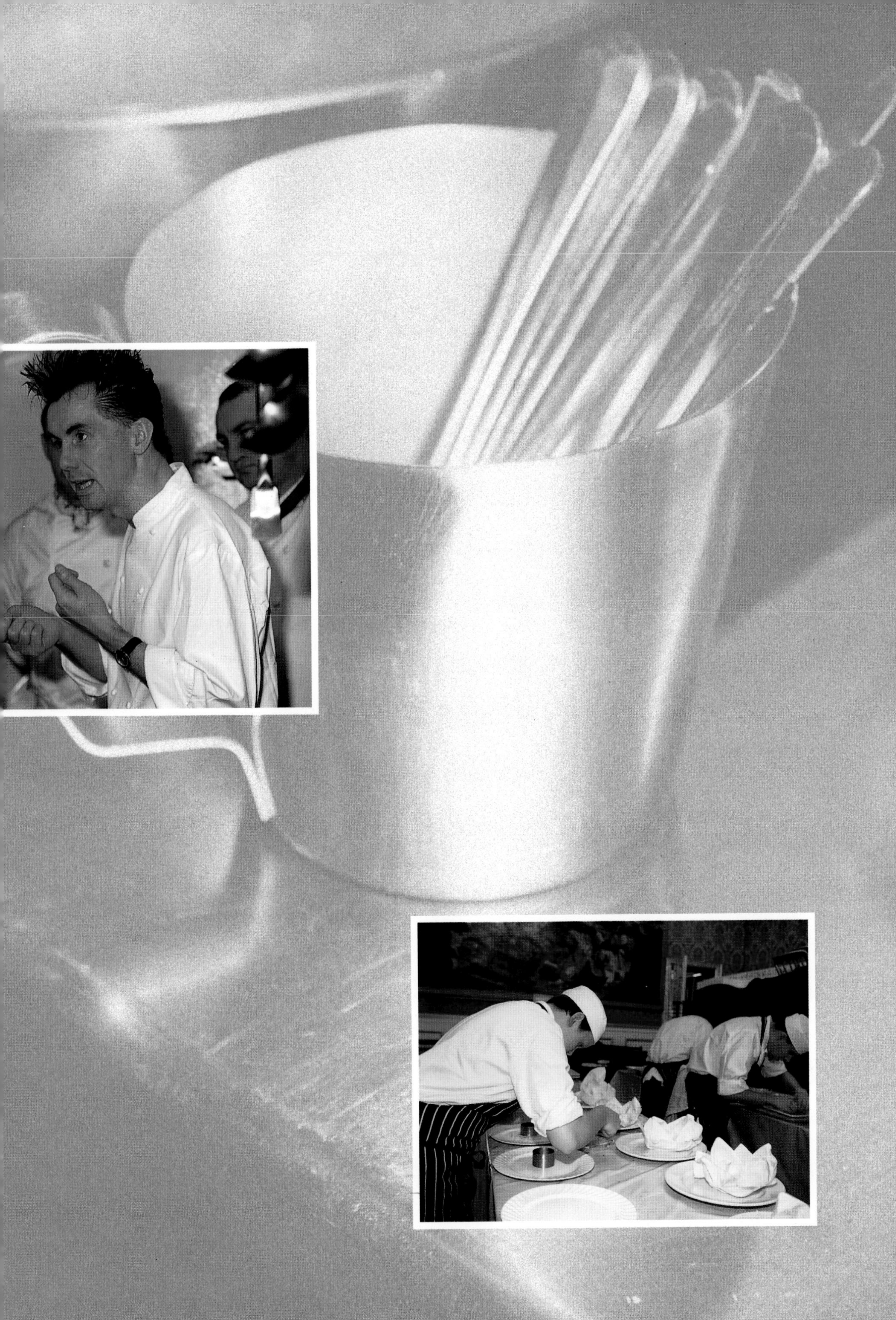

iced vanilla parfait with roasted nutmeg apples

serves 8

The beauty of serving an iced parfait for dessert is that it can be prepared and frozen well in advance. The caramelised apples can also be made in advance, and warmed through before serving. Vanilla pods give an aromatic flavour, with the small black seeds enhancing the appearance of the parfait. If unavailable, replace with 2–3 teaspoons of vanilla essence.

8 egg yolks

225g (8oz) caster sugar

2 vanilla pods, split and seeds scraped out, or 2–3 teaspoons vanilla essence

600ml (1 pint) double cream

4 Granny Smiths or Golden Delicious apples, peeled, quartered and cored

knob of butter

2–3 teaspoons demerara or caster sugar

1/2 teaspoon freshly grated nutmeg

150ml (¼ pint) clotted cream, to serve (optional)

for the caramelised melba toast

2 slices medium-sliced bread

icing sugar

Line a 1.3 litre (2¼ pint) terrine or loaf tin, or 8 x 6cm (2½in) ring moulds with cling film or greaseproof paper.

Whisk together the egg yolks, sugar and vanilla seeds or essence in a heatproof bowl, placed over a pan of simmering water, until it doubles in volume, and reaches the thick ribbon (sabayon) stage. Remove from the heat and whisk until cool (this can be done with an electric mixer).

Lightly whip the double cream until it forms soft peaks. Fold it into the sabayon and pour into the lined terrine or individual ring moulds. Freeze for 2–3 hours.

Meanwhile, make the caramelised melba toasts. Toast the slices on both sides, remove the crusts and split each slice through the middle. Scrape away the crumbs and cut each piece into two triangles. Dust heavily with icing sugar and sit them at the bottom of a grill on low setting. The sugar will slowly caramelise – once it is golden with burnt tinges of sugar, the melbas are ready.

Halve each apple quarter, then place in a pan of cold water and bring to the boil. Drain and dry the apples. When ready to serve, pan-fry the apples in melted butter, adding the sugar and ¼ teaspoon nutmeg, until it starts to caramelise. Add 1–2 tablespoons of water, and cook until the caramel becomes a thick syrup. (Alternatively, dust the apple with caster or icing sugar and caramelise under a hot grill or using a blowtorch, just before serving.)

To serve the parfait, turn it out of the terrine or ring moulds and place on a plate with the apples, as shown. For an extra flavour, serve with nutmeg clotted cream – stir ¼ teaspoon freshly grated nutmeg into 150ml (¼ pint) clotted cream, then refrigerate until set. To serve, shape spoonfuls between two spoons and sit each on top of the parfait. Place a piece of melba toast on top of the clotted cream. Drizzle the caramel over the apples and serve.

alastairlittle

Alastair Little is a self-taught chef who refuses to be influenced by current fads and fashions. He opened his first, much acclaimed restaurant – Alastair Little – in London's Soho before adding another branch in London's Lancaster Road, for which he received and continues to receive critical acclaim. Alastair is a regular on television and has written, together with Richard Whittington, a number of cookery books, including *Keep It Simple* which won the Glenfiddich Book of the Year Award in 1994 and *Food From The Sun*. Alastair also teaches cookery at La Cacciata in Umbria, Italy.

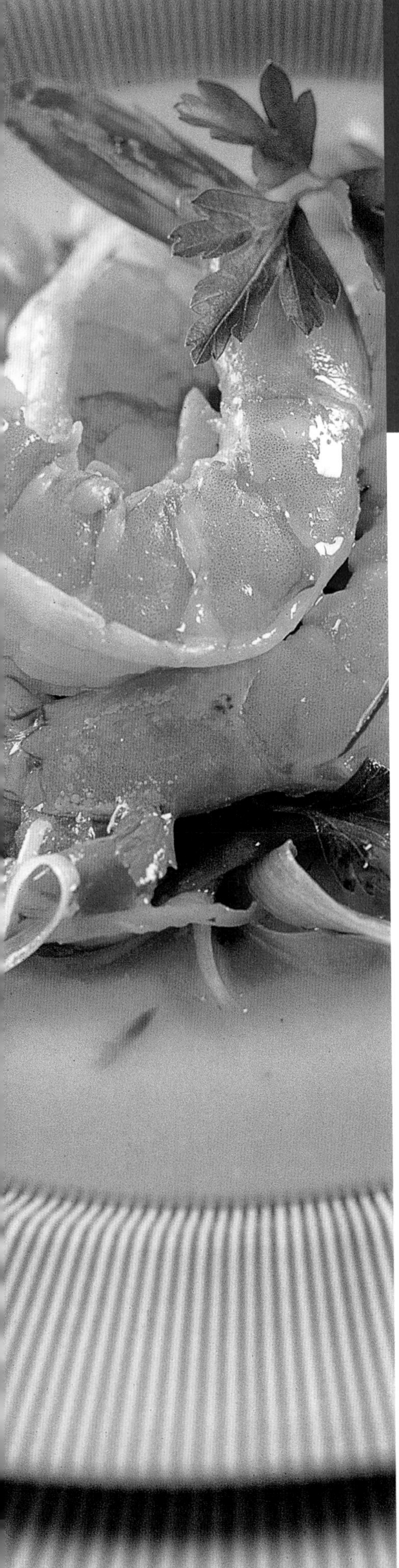

alastairlittle

menu

appetizer
filo-wrapped asparagus & prosciutto

fish course
tiger prawn chermoula sauté

second course
spinach & ricotta risotto

main course
chicken breast stuffed with porcini mushrooms

dessert
apple, prune & zabaglione tart

Reebok Stadium, Bolton

wines

white

Gewürztraminer, Cave Vinicole de Ribeauvillé 1997, France

Gewürztraminer is a distinctively perfumed, exotic, spicy varietal for which Alsace is best known. The pungent melon and lychee bouquet and slightly off-dry palate make a splendid match for spices like paprika, cumin and kaffir lime leaves, all present in this slightly sweet Moroccan-styled tiger prawn dish.

Gavi, S. Orsola 1998, Italy

Piedmonte's most celebrated and best white wine. Brilliant straw-yellow colour, soft, delicate and appealing bouquet with the dry, fresh and persuasive taste of the Cortese grape. The high acidity contrasts with the rich, creamy risotto, while the delicate, minerally quality of the wine complements the light flavours of the ricotta cheese.

red

Valpolicella Classico Superiore, Domini Veneti
Negrar 1997, Italy

Made from Corvina, Rondinella and Molinara grapes, Valpolicella is one of the most popular red wines in the Veneto. The wine is firm, deep and fruity with a slight bitter cherry twist on the finish. A fantastic match with the full-flavoured porcini and chicken, with just enough tannin to match the weight of the dish.

dessert

Asti, Spumante, S. Orsola NV, Italy

The elegant, yet richly fruity bouquet of this superb Asti is matched by a deliciously concentrated flavour on the palate and a stylish, grapey acidity on the finish. The lightness of the wine (only 7.5 per cent ABV) and frothy palate match the light zabaglione element of the dish, while the single fruit note of grapes adds to the apple and prune flavours.

alastairlittle

filo-wrapped asparagus & prosciutto

2 cloves garlic, finely chopped

50g (2oz) butter

8 sheets filo pastry

50g (2oz) Parmesan, finely grated

freshly ground black pepper

8 thin slices Parma ham

8 asparagus spears, trimmed

1 lemon, quartered, to serve

In a small saucepan, sauté the garlic in the butter over a low heat for 10 minutes. Remove from the heat and leave for a further 10 minutes to allow the flavour of the garlic to infuse the butter. Pass through a fine sieve into a bowl and discard the garlic.

Preheat the oven to 230°C/450°F/ Gas Mark 8. Working one sheet at a time, and keeping the sheets not in use under a damp tea towel, spread out each sheet of filo and brush with the garlic butter, then fold in half. Sprinkle with the Parmesan and pepper but no salt (remember that the ham is salty).

Lay a slice of the ham on top of the filo, then place an asparagus spear across and roll up.

Brush the filo roll with more butter, then cut it into 5cm (2in) lengths and place on a non-stick baking tray. Repeat with the remaining ingredients. Bake for 10 minutes, until nicely golden.

Serve 2 rolls per person, with a lemon quarter on the side.

tiger prawn chermoula sauté

Chermoula is the aromatic spice mix that is commonly used in Moroccan cookery. It enhances any fish or chicken dish and here turns prawns into a great first course. The dish works equally well as a main course served with rice or maybe a rocket salad.

4 ripe plum tomatoes

450g (1lb) raw tiger prawns, in the shell

2 teaspoons light plain white flour

salt and freshly ground black pepper

2 teaspoons ground cumin

1 teaspoon paprika

1 glass (150ml/¼ pint) dry white wine

1 fresh kaffir lime leaf

10 whole black peppercorns

12 saffron strands

6 tablespoons extra-virgin olive oil

8 spring onions, cut into julienne strips, about 2cm (¾in) long

2 cloves garlic, chopped

4cm (1½in) piece of fresh root ginger, cut into julienne strips

1 hot chilli, deseeded and cut into thin strips

juice of ½ lemon

bunch of fresh flat-leaf parsley, stalks removed and leaves chopped, reserving a few whole, to garnish

bunch of fresh coriander, stalks removed and leaves chopped

Plunge the tomatoes into a small saucepan of boiling water for 30 seconds, refresh in ice-cold water and peel. Halve the tomatoes, discard the seeds and scoop out the pulp and reserve. Dice the flesh and reserve.

Head and shell the prawns, leaving the tail on and reserving the trimmings. Devein the prawns. Put the prawns in a bag with the flour, 1 teaspoon each of salt and pepper, the cumin and the paprika. Toss well to coat.

Put the reserved prawn heads and shells in a small saucepan with the white wine, tomato pulp, lime leaf and peppercorns. Bring to the boil, reduce the heat and bubble gently for 15 minutes. Strain into a separate pan and reduce the liquid over a high heat to about 4 tablespoons. Remove from the heat and add the saffron threads to the reduced liquid to infuse.

Heat the oil in a large, heavy-based frying pan over a medium heat. When it is hot but not smoking, add the spring onions, garlic, diced tomato, the ginger and chilli and stir-fry for 1 minute.

Add the saffron stock and the lemon juice and stir vigorously. Turn off the heat and stir in the chopped parsley (reserving the whole leaves, to garnish) and coriander. Taste and season with a little more salt, if necessary.

Meanwhile, fry the prawns for about 2 minutes on both sides, until pink and just cooked.

To serve, put the spring onion mixture in 4 deep plates, arrange the prawns on top and scatter with the reserved parsley.

alastairlittle

spinach & ricotta risotto

serves 4–6

125g (4½oz) butter

1 large onion, very finely chopped

300g (10½oz) arborio (risotto) rice

100g (4oz) picked spinach, washed thoroughly

50g (2oz) ricotta

75g (3oz) Parmesan, freshly grated

for the stock

2 carrots, peeled

2 sticks of celery, peeled

2 onions, peeled

1 bay leaf

salt and freshly ground black pepper

To make the stock, pulse the vegetables in a food processor until finely chopped. Put the vegetables and bay leaf in a large saucepan and cover with water, at least 4 litres (6¾ pints). Season and bring to the boil. Boil for 30 minutes, then pass through a sieve. Discard the vegetables and return the stock to the boil, reducing it to concentrate the flavour, until you are left with about 2 litres (3¼ pints). Allow to cool and refrigerate if not using immediately.

To make the risotto, heat the stock to a simmer. Melt half the butter in a heavy-based saucepan and add the onion. Sweat over a medium heat for 5 minutes, until softened. Add the rice and sweat, stirring, until the rice starts to stick to the base of the pan.

Add 2 ladles of stock. Cook, stirring, until the liquid has been absorbed and the rice becomes sticky. Continue adding ladles of stock, allowing the rice to absorb the liquid before each addition and stirring continuously.

When the rice is creamy and just tender, turn off the heat and fold in the spinach, the remaining butter, ricotta and the grated Parmesan. Season to taste, stir, cover, and leave for 3 minutes before serving.

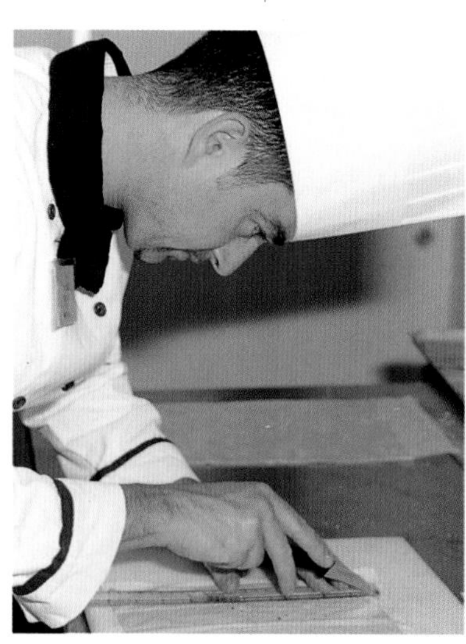

chicken breast stuffed with porcini mushrooms

2 chicken crowns (preferably free-range or corn-fed)

salt and freshly ground black pepper

25g (1oz) caul fat, soaked in cold water for 3 hours

450g (1lb) Savoy cabbage, shredded and blanched

75g (3oz) pancetta, cut into strips

for the stuffing

10g (1/3oz) butter

1/2 onion, finely diced

25g (1oz) dried porcini, soaked in warm water for 1 hour and chopped, soaking liquor reserved

for the sauce

1 tablespoon oil

1 onion, diced

1 carrot, diced

1 stick of celery, diced

1 bay leaf

1/2 tablespoon red wine vinegar

1 teaspoon caster sugar

100ml (3 1/2fl oz) white wine

for the garlic butter

25g (1oz) butter

1 clove garlic, finely chopped

1 handful fresh flat-leaf parsley, coarsely chopped

juice of 1 lemon

First make the stuffing: melt the butter in a heavy-based frying pan and sweat the onion until translucent. Add half the porcini and sweat for 5 minutes. Add the strained porcini liquor, increase the heat and cook until the liquid has evaporated. Check the seasoning and leave to cool.

Remove the backbone and wing tips from the crowns, chop and reserve for the sauce. Carefully pull the skin back from the crowns and spread the stuffing under, then pull the skin back over the stuffing and season well. Wrap the stuffed crowns in a layer of caul fat.

To make the sauce, heat the oil in a saucepan and add the chopped bones and trimmings. Sauté until they have browned and start to stick to the bottom of the pan, then add the vegetables. Reduce the heat and continue to cook for about 15 minutes, until the vegetables have softened. Add the vinegar and sugar, increase the heat and cook for about 2 minutes, until the trimmings and vegetables have caramelised and are deep brown in colour.

Add the wine and continue to cook the sauce over a high heat, until the liquid has almost evaporated. Add enough water to barely cover the trimmings and vegetables, then continue to boil vigorously for about 30 minutes, until the liquid has evaporated. Add more water to barely cover the trimmings and vegetables, and skim off any fat. Reduce the heat to medium and cook for 1 hour, until the liquid has reduced by half. Allow to cool a little, then strain into a small pan.

Combine the ingredients for the garlic butter and add to the sauce. Reheat until smooth and glossy.

Meanwhile, roast the chicken crowns in an oven preheated to 200°C/400°F/Gas Mark 6, for 45 minutes, until browned. Allow them to rest for 10 minutes, then carve, cutting through the bone.

Sauté the pancetta and reserved porcini in a little oil, then add the cabbage and cook until softened.

Serve the chicken on a bed of the cabbage mixture and spoon around the sauce.

apple, prune & zabaglione tart

serves 6–8

12 prunes

1 Lapsang Souchong teabag

75g (3oz) caster sugar

6 large, tart eating apples, peeled, cored and segmented

75g (3oz) butter

2 tablespoons Calvados

for the pastry

350g (12oz) plain flour

pinch of salt

75g (3oz) icing sugar

175g (6oz) unsalted butter, cut into small pieces

2 eggs

for the zabaglione

100g (4oz) butter

2 eggs

100g (4oz) caster sugar

2 drops vanilla essence

1 tablespoon Calvados

First prepare the prunes: make the tea, sweeten with 2 teaspoons of sugar and soak the prunes in the liquid. Leave for 30 minutes, until plump, then stone the prunes and leave to cool.

Part-cook the apples with the butter and the rest of the sugar in a frying pan, gradually drizzling over the Calvados. Leave to cool.

To make the pastry shell, sift the flour, salt and sugar into a bowl. Add the butter and rub with your fingertips until the mixture forms fine breadcrumbs. Make a well in the centre of the mixture, add the eggs and mix with a knife to form crumbs. Press the crumbs together with your fingers. Knead lightly for a few seconds, then form into a ball.

Wrap with cling film and leave to rest in the refrigerator for 30 minutes. Roll out the dough and use to line a 25cm (10in) tart tin. Line the pastry shell with greaseproof paper and then with a double sheet of foil. Fill the pastry shell with dried beans to weight it down. Press down firmly and return it to the refrigerator for 30 minutes. Preheat the oven to 200°C/400°F/Gas Mark 6.

Put the pastry shell on a baking tray and bake for 10 minutes, until the visible rim of the pastry starts to brown. Remove from the oven and gingerly lift off the foil and beans, then peel away the greaseproof paper. Return the pastry to the oven and bake for a further 5 minutes. Remove and leave to cool. Reduce the oven to 180°C/350°F/Gas Mark 4.

When the apples and prunes have cooled, arrange them in the pastry case, but do not overfill it as you need to leave room for the custard topping – no more than three-quarters of the way up.

For the zabaglione, melt the butter in a saucepan over a very low heat. In a large bowl, beat the eggs with the sugar until stiff. Then, continuing to beat, pour in the hot melted butter in a thin stream, followed by the vanilla essence and Calvados. Transfer the zabaglione to a jug and return the tart to the oven on the baking tray. When the tart is in place in the oven, carefully pour the zabaglione over the apples and prunes, making sure it does not run down the sides of the pastry.

Bake for 15 minutes, until the top is golden brown but the inside is still slightly liquid. Cut into slices and serve warm.

tonytobin

Tony Tobin began his career at the Capital Hotel working under Brian Turner. This was followed by five years under Nico Landenis, culminating in Tony becoming Head Chef at A Very Simply Nico. At the age of 25, Tony took over as Head Chef at the South Lodge Hotel in Lower Beding, winning the *Good Food Guide*'s County Restaurant of the Year award. At present Tony is the Executive Chef at the Dining Room in Reigate and has recently opened Dining Room 2 in Haywards Heath. He is also the director of a fast-growing chain of Italian restaurants called Tortellini's based in and around south London. Tony is a regular on the BBC series *Ready, Steady Cook*. He is also spokesperson for Chef and Brewer Pubs as part of his campaign to inspire young people to enter into the catering industry.

tonytobin

menu

starter

lasagne of marinated salmon with lemon dressing & chive oil

fish course

hot & sweet scallops with sticky rice & crab chopsticks

main course

fillet of rabbit roasted in parma ham with fennel confit & chorizo oil

dessert

raspberry clafoutis in a sweet pastry box with a lemon sabayon

Kenley House, Surrey

wines

white

Pinot Bianco, Colli Berici, Casa de Fra 1998, Italy

A fresh, easy-drinking wine with a crisp, lemony character, from the gentle hilly countryside around Verona. Like many northern Italian white wines, it has a high acidity that is perfect for cutting through food with a high oil content, such as this rich salmon lasagne.

Oxford Landing Limited Release Viognier, Yalumba 1998, Australia

An exotic, dry, unoaked white using the rare Viognier grape, and full of the typical apricot, peach and lychee flavours associated with this varietal. A terrific flavour match with the hot, sweet scallops.

red

Tempranillo, Masia Bach, Penedés 1996, Spain

A rich, flavoursome, oak-matured red wine using Spain's premier grape, the Tempranillo, with ripe fruit and firm tannins. This wine has plenty of tannins to complement the richness of the rabbit and bacon, and a spicy nature that matches the hot chorizo oil.

dessert

Sancerre Rosé, Le Rabault, Joseph Mellot 1998, France

Pure Pinot Noir, lightly macerated on the grapeskins to produce a fragrant and rich dry rosé, with a hint of strawberries on the nose and palate. An unusual dry selection for a dessert wine, that nevertheless works extremely well due to the summer fruit notes and refreshing acidity.

lasagne of marinated salmon with lemon dressing & chive oil

225g (8oz) salmon, sliced thinly lengthways

juice of 1/2 lemon and 1/2 lime

1 tablespoon white wine vinegar

1 tablespoon icing sugar

100ml (3fl oz) olive oil

125ml (4fl oz) balsamic vinegar

salad leaves, to garnish

for the pasta

2 eggs

3 egg yolks

550g (1lb 4oz) farino "O" flour

pinch of salt

oil, for brushing

for the chive oil

1 large bunch chives, chopped

150ml (¼ pint) olive oil

To make the pasta, mix the eggs and yolks together in a bowl. Make a well in the centre of the flour and add the egg mixture. Draw the flour into the eggs until it resembles breadcrumbs. Whizz briefly in a food processor.

Allow to rest, covered with a dampened tea towel, for 1 hour. Then, using a pasta machine, roll the pasta into thin sheets. Trim them into 20 lengths, each 12.5cm (5in) long.

Cook the sheets, a few at a time, for 1–2 minutes in boiling, salted water to which a splash of oil has been added. Drain, refresh, pat dry and brush the sheets with a little oil.

Marinate the salmon in the lemon and lime juice for 2–3 minutes, then season with salt and pepper.

Brush a tray with oil and line with cling film. Layer the pasta and salmon, starting with a sheet of pasta, followed by a layer of salmon, until you have 5 pasta layers and 4 salmon layers. Continue to create 4 portions. Reserve any citrus juice for the dressing. Cover with cling film, refrigerate, and allow to set for at least 2 hours.

Make a citrus dressing with the reserved lemon and lime juice, the white wine vinegar, icing sugar and olive oil. Blend in a food processor until combined.

Make the chive oil by blending the chives with the olive oil. Season with salt and freshly ground black pepper.

Put the balsamic vinegar into a pan, bring to the boil and cook until reduced to a syrup.

Remove the tray from the refrigerator, remove the cling film and, using a sharp knife, trim the salmon lasagnes into 4 neat, even portions, each approximately 11cm (4½in) x 7.5cm (3in).

Serve garnished with salad leaves. Drizzle around the balsamic syrup, chive oil and citrus dressing.

tonytobin

hot & sweet scallops with sticky rice & crab chopsticks

1 teaspoon finely diced fresh root ginger

1 dessertspoon olive oil

400g (14oz) crabmeat

salt and freshly ground black pepper

8 spring roll wrappers

beaten egg, to glaze

200g (7oz) Thai fragrant rice

100ml (3½fl oz) coconut milk

1 dessertspoon lime juice

4 large scallops, slashed

oil, for frying

for the hot & sweet sauce

2.5cm (1in) piece of fresh root ginger, grated

1 red chilli, finely diced

1 clove garlic, chopped

zest of 1 lime

200ml (7fl oz) white wine vinegar

200g (7oz) caster sugar

Sweat the ginger in half the olive oil until softened. Add the crabmeat and season with salt and pepper. Allow to cool.

Brush the spring roll wrappers with a little egg wash. Place a little of the crab mixture in the centre of each one and roll into a thin chopstick shape. Set aside. Reserve the remaining crabmeat.

Boil the rice in twice its volume of salty water. Cover and simmer until all the liquid has evaporated. Add the coconut milk and simmer until the rice is tender. Check the seasoning and add the lime juice.

Place the ingredients for the sauce in a pan and bring to the boil, then reduce the heat and simmer for 10 minutes. Leave to cool then liquidise.

Heat enough oil in a pan to deep-fry the chopsticks, then fry until crisp and golden.

Meanwhile, heat a heavy-based frying pan with the rest of the olive oil. Sear the scallops briefly, making sure they are still rare in the centre. Season to taste.

Serve the scallops on a bed of the remaining crabmeat. Drizzle the sauce over the scallops and serve with a spoonful of rice and the crabsticks.

tonytobin

fillet of rabbit roasted in parma ham with fennel confit & chorizo oil

1 chorizo sausage, finely chopped

360ml (12fl oz) olive oil

4 rabbit middle fillets, each about 150g (5oz)

4 slices of Parma ham

1 bulb of fennel, trimmed and quartered

zest of 1 orange

1 clove garlic, chopped

1 teaspoon caster sugar

salt and freshly ground black pepper

450g (1lb) potatoes, peeled and cut into dice

25ml (1fl oz) truffle oil

175ml (6fl oz) balsamic vinegar

Preheat the oven to 200°C/400°F/ Gas Mark 6. Fry the chorizo in a pan with a little olive oil for about 10 minutes, or until caramelised. Add 200ml (7fl oz) of the oil, simmer for 30 minutes and leave to cool. Pass through a fine strainer, discarding the chorizo, and set aside.

Season the rabbit with a little salt and pepper and wrap each fillet in a slice of the Parma ham.

Place the fennel in an earthenware dish, add the orange zest, garlic, sugar and cover with olive oil. Roast in the oven for 90 minutes, until the fennel is tender. Remove from the oven and keep the fennel warm.

Heat a little oil in a large frying pan and fry the rabbit until golden on all sides, then place in the oven for a further 5 minutes. Remove and keep warm.

Cook the potatoes in boiling water for 15 minutes, until tender, then mash with the truffle oil.

Put the balsamic vinegar into a pan and bring to the boil and cook until it has reduced by two-thirds.

Pipe a little of the truffle mash onto 4 plates, lean a piece of fennel up against it and top with a rabbit fillet. Drizzle around a little of the chorizo oil and balsamic syrup.

tonytobin

raspberry clafoutis in a sweet pastry box with a lemon sabayon

for the pastry

150g (5oz) unsalted butter
100g (4oz) caster sugar
40g (1½oz) icing sugar, sifted
375g (13oz) soft flour, sifted
pinch of salt, sifted
2 egg yolks
1 egg
2 tablespoons cream
2 tablespoons fondant icing
400g (14oz) fresh raspberries
icing sugar, to decorate
fresh sprigs of mint, to decorate

for the clafoutis

400ml (14fl oz) double cream
1 vanilla pod
3 egg yolks
50g (2oz) sugar
1 leaf of gelatine, pre-soaked

for the lemon sabayon

200g (7oz) caster sugar
100ml (3½fl oz) water
juice and zest of 3 lemons
3 egg yolks

for the raspberry coulis

300g (12oz) raspberries
100g (4oz) caster sugar
juice of ¼ lemon

To make the pastry, place the butter, sugars, flour and salt in a food processor and pulse until just combined. Add the egg yolks, whole egg and cream and pulse until it comes together (do not overmix). Turn the dough out and form into a ball. Cover the pastry with cling film and chill for 45–60 minutes before using.

Roll out the pastry until about 3mm (⅛in) thick. Score the pastry using the back of a knife to form 8 x 7cm (2¾in) squares and 16 x 4cm (1½in) deep and 7cm (2¾in) wide pieces. Chill and allow to rest. Cut the pastry into the marked pieces and allow to cool. Brush the pastry with egg white and dust with icing sugar, then bake in an oven preheated to 200°C/400°F/ Gas Mark 6 for 10 minutes, until crisp and light golden.

Gently warm the fondant icing in a small pan and spoon into a small piping bag. Pipe a thin line of fondant down the short edges of the rectangles and carefully press 4 rectangles together to form the sides of a box. Allow to dry for about 2 hours. Repeat with the remaining rectangles.

Place the raspberries into a plastic tray, reserving a few to decorate.

To make the clafoutis, put the cream and vanilla pod into a pan and bring to the boil. Pour the mixture over the yolks, whisking continuously. Add the sugar, return to the pan and cook gently until the custard coats the back of a spoon – do not allow it to boil. Remove from the heat, add the gelatine, stir to dissolve and strain the mixture over the raspberries. Allow to cool and then refrigerate until set.

To make the lemon sabayon, combine the sugar, water, lemon juice and zest in a pan and bring to the boil. Cook until the mixture starts to thicken, then pour it over the egg yolks and whisk until cold.

To make the raspberry coulis, purée the raspberries and sugar in a blender, pass through a sieve and add the lemon juice.

To serve, place a pastry box in the centre of a serving plate and spoon some of the raspberry clafoutis in the box and top with the lemon sabayon. Place a square pastry lid on top. Dust with icing sugar and decorate with fresh raspberries and mint. Spoon the raspberry coulis around the outside.

nicknairn

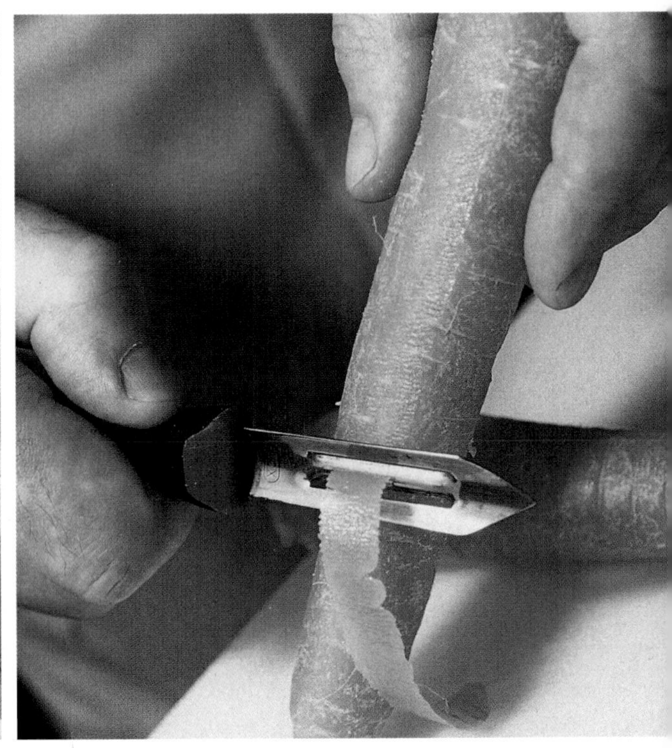

Nick Nairn is self-taught and the youngest chef to win a highly acclaimed Michelin star in Scotland. Keen to promote his Scottish roots, he became a founder member of the Scottish Chef's Association. In 1997 he opened Nairns Restaurant, which was instantly acclaimed by the national press as the hottest restaurant in Scotland. His television credits are numerous, including two series of the BBC's *Wild Harvest* as well as appearing regularly on *Ready Steady Cook* and *Who'll do The Pudding?*

nicknairn

menu

starter

hot smoked salmon with avocado salsa

soup course

a minestrone of shellfish

main course

roast leg of lamb with garlic, rosemary, roasted baby plum tomatoes & broad bean "stew"

dessert

whisky parfait with agen prunes & earl grey syrup

Cutlers Hall, Sheffield

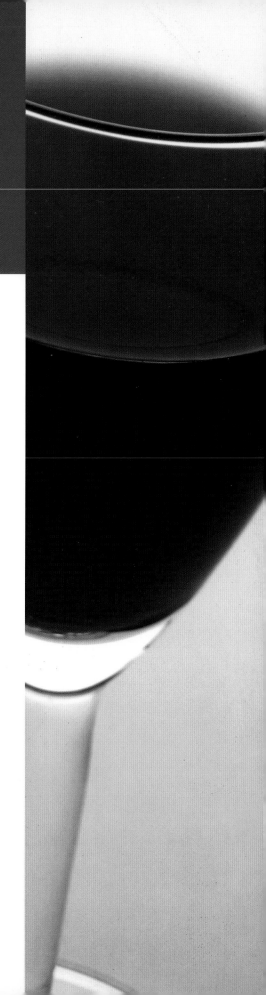

wines

white

Oyster Bay Sauvignon Blanc, Delegat's Estate 1999, New Zealand

A fine, dry white, with the freshness and assertive grassy aroma of well-made Sauvignon Blanc, a crisp juicy acidity and the unique intensity of Marlborough-grown fruit. A superb match for most fish, Sauvignon Blanc provides both attractive herbaceous flavours and a cutting acidity which cleanses the mouth ready for the next bite.

Chardonnay Reserve, Sliven 1997, Bulgaria

This white wine is straw coloured with a greenish tinge. It is rich, buttery and full-flavoured with good fruit and balance, benefiting from six months maturation in American oak. An excellent if unusual selection, which really enhances the soup by providing both spicy, creamy flavours and a contrasting weighty mouthfeel.

red

Château de France 1996, Graves, France

Up and coming château, utilising a 60 per cent Merlot and 40 per cent Cabernet Sauvignon blend, which is matured in new oak barriques. The plum and blackcurrant fruit character, intensity of flavour and noticeable tannins all complement the rich, quite fatty, roasted lamb. Rosemary is one of the few herbs that matches well with a full-bodied wine.

dessert

Chivas Regal, Scotch Whisky

This smooth, top class blend of whiskys – all over 12 years old – is an obvious choice for matching with the whisky parfait. Not only does it complement the parfait, but also the smoky tones of the earl grey syrup. It could be lightened slightly with a splash of water.

nicknairn

hot smoked salmon with avocado salsa

300g (10½oz) hot smoked salmon, flaked

4 tablespoons balsamic vinegar

mixed baby organic salad leaves, dressed with olive oil and lemon juice, to garnish

for the red pepper oil

1 large red pepper

200ml (7fl oz) olive oil

for the herb oil

a handful each of flat-leaf parsley and dill

150ml (¼ pint) olive oil

for the avocado salsa

1 large avocado, peeled and diced

2 plum tomatoes, diced

½ small red onion, diced

1 red chilli, finely chopped

1 dessertspoon Japanese pickled ginger (sushi ginger), finely chopped

2 tablespoons chopped fresh coriander

1 tablespoon Thai fish sauce

2 tablespoons lime juice

Maldon salt and freshly ground white pepper

The pepper oil should be made 24 hours in advance of serving. Roast the pepper in an oven preheated to 200°C/400°F/Gas Mark 6 until blackened all over. Peel the pepper, remove the seeds, and roughly chop.

In a large pan, heat the chopped pepper in the olive oil and simmer gently for 5 minutes. Blend the mixture until puréed, then leave to cool and pass through a sieve.

To make the herb oil, blend the herbs and olive oil until puréed.

To prepare the salsa, combine all the ingredients in a bowl, mix well and leave for 1 hour to allow the flavours to infuse.

Meanwhile, make the balsamic syrup. Put the balsamic vinegar in a saucepan and heat until reduced by half and syrupy.

To serve, place a 7.5cm (3in) ring mould in the centre of a serving plate. Place the salmon in the base of each ring and arrange it up the sides so that it holds the salsa. Arrange the salsa inside the salmon round and remove the ring mould. Pile salad leaves on top and drizzle the herb oil, red pepper oil and the balsamic syrup around. Repeat to make 4 servings.

a minestrone of shellfish

- 900ml (1 1/2 pints) fish stock
- 2 fresh Scottish scallops
- 4 Scottish langoustine
- 12 mussels, cleaned
- 2 tablespoons olive oil
- 2 rashers smoked streaky bacon, cut into lardons
- 1 onion, chopped
- 1 clove garlic, chopped
- 2 plum tomatoes, chopped
- 300ml (1/2 pint) passata
- 150ml (1/4 pint) white wine
- 1 courgette, diced
- 25g (1oz) very small dried pasta shells
- Maldon salt and freshly ground white pepper
- fresh basil, shredded, to garnish
- Parmesan shavings, to garnish

Heat 300ml (½ pint) of the fish stock and briefly poach the scallops and langoustines. Remove from the stock, halve the scallops, peel and halve the langoustines, and reserve both. Steam the mussels briefly until the shells have opened – discard any that have not opened. Remove from the shells.

Heat the oil in a large saucepan and fry the bacon until crisp. Add the onion and garlic and sweat until softened. Add the tomatoes, passata and wine. Add the fish stock and poaching liquor and cook for 10 minutes.

Add the courgette and pasta shells, then continue to cook until the pasta is tender. Add the shellfish, season to taste and heat through.

Garnish with Parmesan and basil before serving.

t leg of lamb with garlic, rosemary, roasted baby plum tomatoes & broad bean "stew"

Choose dark-fleshed lamb with a good covering of white, firm fat that will add flavour and help to keep the roast moist in the fierce heat of the oven.

To make an excellent gravy from the lamb cooking juices, discard any fat, and add a little wine or water to the roasting tin. Bring to the boil and cook, scraping the sticky bits from the base of the tin. Taste, season, and you will have a rich gravy to spoon over the meat.

serves 6

1.75kg (4lb) leg of lamb

olive oil

2–3 large sprigs of fresh rosemary, divided into small sprigs

4 large cloves garlic, cut into thick slivers or sticks

freshly ground black pepper

Preheat the oven to 220°C/425°F/Gas Mark 7. Using a sharp knife, score the lamb, about 2cm (¾in) deep, in a wide criss-cross pattern. Rub the whole leg with a good slug of olive oil and place in a roasting tin. Tuck as much rosemary and garlic into the criss-cross cuts as you like. Season with plenty of black pepper. If you have any rosemary left over, tuck it well under the meat, where it will give lots of flavour and will not burn.

Place the lamb in the oven and sear for 15 minutes, then reduce the heat to 180°C/350°F/Gas Mark 4 and roast for a further 1 hour, basting the meat from time to time. (The lamb should be well-cooked on the outside with crunchy bits, and rosy pink near the bone.) Remove the meat from the oven, transfer to a warm carving dish, cover loosely with foil, and leave to rest in a warm place for 15 minutes before carving.

roasted baby plum tomatoes & broad bean "stew"

Baby vegetables are generally pretty tasteless, but these little tomatoes are packed with flavour. Baby broad beans add the finishing spring touch with a dash of green and their sweet, young flavour.

700g (1¾lb) broad beans in the pod to give about 350g (12oz) beans, or frozen broad beans, shelled

625g (1lb 5oz) baby plum tomatoes

4 tablespoons olive oil

Maldon salt and freshly ground black pepper

2 sprigs of fresh thyme

Blanch the beans in boiling water for 1 minute. Drain and plunge into a bowl of cold water to cool them down quickly. Drain and pop them out of their skins. (If using frozen beans, cook in boiling water for 2–3 minutes and do exactly the same as for the fresh ones.)

Place the tomatoes in a roasting tin, pour over the olive oil and season with salt and pepper. Add the thyme.

Roast with the lamb for about 20 minutes, or until the tomatoes have slightly collapsed and the skins are beginning to brown.

Whip them out of the oven and mix in the beans, pop back in the oven for a few minutes to heat up the beans. Serve with the lamb.

whisky parfait with agen prunes & earl grey syrup

4 egg yolks

300ml (1/2 pint) double cream

100g (4oz) caster sugar

for the earl grey prunes

300ml (1/2 pint) water

25g (1oz) sugar

1 tablespoon Earl Grey tea leaves

16 Agen prunes

1/2 tablespoon lemon juice

3 tablespoons Chivas Regal

First prepare the prunes: bring the water and sugar to the boil. Add the tea leaves and allow to infuse for 6 minutes. Pass the syrup through a sieve into a bowl, and add the prunes to the hot liquid. Add the lemon juice and half of the Chivas Regal. Leave to cool, then marinate the prunes in the refrigerator overnight – longer if desired.

To make the parfait, whisk the egg yolks in an electric mixer until very pale and increased in volume. Whip the cream with the rest of the Chivas Regal until it starts to thicken.

Bring the caster sugar and 1 1/2 tablespoons of water to the boil in a saucepan. Boil until it reaches the softball stage. (To find out if it is ready, dip a cold teaspoon in the syrup to coat it. Dip the spoon into cold water to set and pinch a little between finger and thumb. When the mixture can be rolled into a soft ball it is ready.)

With a mixer running on full speed, slowly pour the softball sugar over the whisked egg yolks. Reduce the speed by half and whisk for a further 5 minutes.

Fold together the egg yolk mixture and the whipped cream and pour into 4 x 125ml (4fl oz) dariole moulds. Freeze immediately. (You could also pour the parfait mixture into a tub and freeze it.)

Remove the parfait from the freezer, run the tip of a knife around each one, invert the moulds and give them a good tap on a surface to release each one.

Serve with the prunes and drizzle around the syrup.

jamesmartin

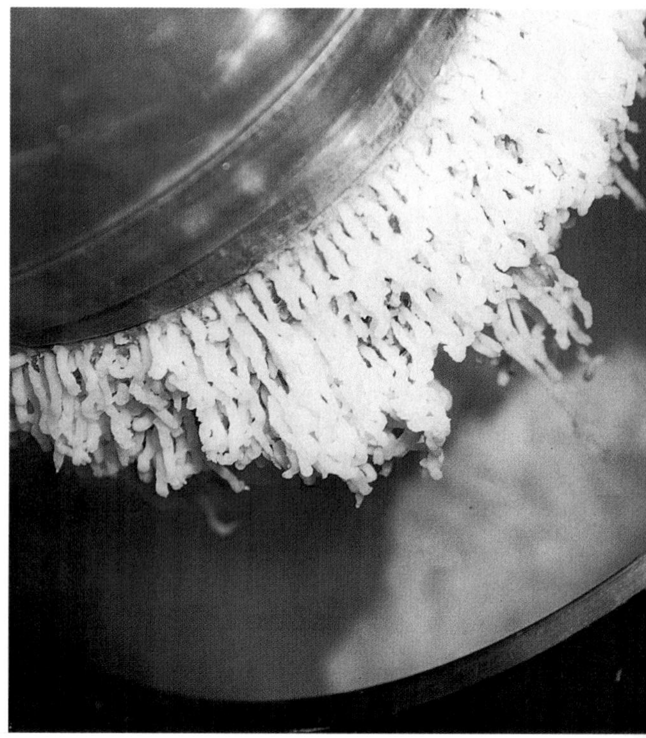

James Martin describes his cooking as "modern British with a hint of Mediterranean" and his flavours are certainly simple and direct but always innovative and challenging. At the tender age of 22, James opened the Hotel & Bistro du Vin in Winchester as head chef. His television career began in 1996 with appearances on BBC's *Ready Steady Cook* and he has gone on to appear on numerous other shows, including *Master Chef*, *Food & Drink* and *Light Lunch*. James also writes a regular recipe column for *Ideal Home* magazine and has written his own book, *Eating in with James Martin,* for the publisher Mitchell Beazley.

jamesmartin

menu

appetizer

yorkshire pudding with foie gras & onion gravy

fish course

seared salmon with rice vermicelli

main course

pan-fried, corn-fed breast of chicken with roasted ceps & jerusalem artichokes

dessert

panna cotta with spiced oranges

Radley College, Oxford

wines

white

Two Vineyards, Chardonnay, Evans & Tate 1997, Australia

A rich, flavoursome Chardonnay, with a toastiness on the palate, from being barrel fermented, and crisp, creamy acidity on the finish. This is a perfectly weighted wine to match the intensely flavoured foie gras and onion gravy. Being a Chardonnay, this wine will also have a good affinity with salmon and most seafood, with enough acidity to contrast with the richness of the fish and any marinade used.

red

Pinot Noir, Vidal Estate 1998, New Zealand

A medium-bodied wine made from the classic Pinot Noir grape, showing typical strawberry fruit flavours and ripe youthful tannins. A year in French oak gives the wine an added structure and complexity. Pinot Noir, with its light tannins and red fruit flavours, is an ideal choice for full-flavoured poultry dishes.

dessert

Muscat de Beaumes de Venise, Caves des Vignerons NV, France

A luscious, sweet, fortified Muscat from the southern Rhône near Avignon. The distinctive perfumed aroma is redolent of elderflower and orange blossom and the sweetness is balanced by an attractive acidity. An extremely versatile dessert wine, which is sweet enough to go with the very sweetest desserts, and a great match with the spiced oranges.

jamesmartin

yorkshire pudding with foie gras & onion gravy

serves 6

225g (8oz) lobe foie gras, sliced

for the Yorkshire puddings

50g (2oz) plain flour

salt and freshly ground black pepper

2 eggs

150ml (1/4 pint) milk

25g (1oz) dripping

for the onion gravy

1 tablespoon vegetable oil

2 red onions, sliced

1 clove garlic, finely chopped

250ml (8fl oz) red wine

475ml (16fl oz) fresh chicken stock

25g (1oz) butter

First make the Yorkshire pudding batter 24 hours in advance: place the flour and seasoning in a bowl, then add the eggs and mix slowly to prevent lumps forming. Stir in the milk and leave overnight in the refrigerator to rest.

Preheat the oven to 220°C/425°F/Gas Mark 7. Divide the dripping between a 6-hole Yorkshire pudding tin and place in the oven until very hot. Remove the tray from the oven and carefully pour in the batter. Return to the oven and bake for 30–40 minutes, until risen and crisp.

To make the onion gravy, heat the oil in a pan and fry the onions and garlic until softened. Add the wine and stock, scraping up the residue from the base of the pan to deglaze. Cook over a high heat until reduced by two-thirds and then add the butter and season to taste. Stir until the butter has melted and the sauce is glossy.

In a hot frying pan, briefly sear the slices of foie gras on both sides.

To serve, divide the Yorkshire puddings and slices of foie gras between 6 plates and spoon the gravy around.

seared salmon with rice vermicelli

serves 6

600g (1½lb) salmon, boned with skin on, cut into 6 x 100g (4oz) fillets

6 tablespoons peanut (groundnut) oil

2 cloves garlic, thinly sliced

100ml (3½fl oz) balsamic vinegar

25g (1oz) fresh basil

100ml (3½fl oz) virgin olive oil

for the spice paste

2 red onions, chopped

4 cloves garlic, chopped

2.5cm (1in) piece fresh galangal, chopped

2.5cm (1in) piece of fresh ginger, chopped

2 red chillis, chopped

1 green chilli, chopped

25g (1oz) palm sugar, roughly chopped

3 tablespoons peanut (groundnut) oil

2 teaspoons fish sauce

for the dressing

1 teaspoon peanut oil

2 tablespoon spice paste

4 tablespoons lime juice

1 tablespoon fish sauce

1 teaspoon palm sugar, roughly chopped

for the vermicelli salad

150g (5oz) rice vermicelli

2 red chillies, sliced

4 pink shallots, sliced

3 fresh kaffir lime leaves, finely shredded

2 tablespoons chopped fresh coriander

2 tablespoons chopped fresh basil

First make the spice paste: place the onion, garlic, galangal, ginger and chillies in a blender, then add the sugar, oil and fish sauce. Blend until the mixture forms a fine paste and set aside.

To make the dressing, place the oil in a hot frying pan and add 2 tablespoons of the spice paste, then fry for about 5 minutes. Place in a bowl and stir in the lime juice, fish sauce and sugar, and set aside.

Briefly sear the salmon fillets, skin-side down, in a pan – but do not fully cook them. Place the salmon on a baking tray and spread the remaining spice paste over the fillets, then leave to marinate for 20 minutes.

To make the salad, place the vermicelli in a large bowl and cover with boiling water. Leave for about 15 minutes, until soft. Drain the noodles and combine with the chillies, shallots, lime leaves, coriander and basil, then add the dressing. Mix well.

Preheat the oven to 180°C/350°F/Gas Mark 4. Bake the salmon for 5 minutes. Meanwhile, heat 6 tablespoons of peanut oil and deep-fry the garlic until golden brown – take care not to burn it.

Place the balsamic vinegar in a pan. Bring to the boil and cook until reduced and syrupy.

Place the basil and oil in a blender and blend until puréed.

To serve, arrange the vermicelli salad on serving plates, then sprinkle over the garlic chips. Top with the salmon and drizzle the basil oil and reduced balsamic vinegar around the salad.

jamesmartin

pan-fried, corn-fed breast of chicken with roasted ceps & jerusalem artichokes

serves 6

6 corn-fed chicken breasts, with skin on, each about 225g (8oz)

60g (2¼oz) unsalted butter

50ml (2fl oz) virgin olive oil

3 tablespoons groundnut oil

4 Jerusalem artichokes, peeled, halved, blanched for 4 minutes, then sliced

25g (1oz) dried ceps, soaked for 20 minutes in hot water then drained

1 bunch of fresh flat-leaf parsley

for the sauce

1 tablespoon olive oil

4 shallots, finely chopped

300ml (½ pint) good quality red wine, reduced to 120ml (4fl oz)

600ml (1 pint) fresh chicken stock, reduced to 250ml (8fl oz)

3 tablespoons red wine vinegar

Maldon salt and freshly ground black pepper

for the mash

900g (2lb) Maris Piper potatoes, peeled and quartered

1 vanilla pod

175ml (6fl oz) double cream

175g (6oz) unsalted butter

Preheat the oven to 190°C/375°F/Gas Mark 5. First make the sauce: heat the oil in a saucepan and sauté the shallots until softened. Add the reduced wine and stock, and the vinegar, then bring to the boil. Cook for a few minutes, season to taste, and set aside.

Heat half the butter and olive oil in a frying pan and add the chicken. Cook until sealed and browned, and season with salt and pepper. Place the chicken on a baking tray and roast in the oven for about 15–20 minutes.

Meanwhile, heat half the groundnut oil in a separate frying pan. Add the artichokes and fry over a high heat for about 4 minutes, until golden, then place on kitchen paper to drain. Heat the remaining groundnut oil, add the ceps and fry for about 2 minutes over a high heat. Chop half the parsley and add it to the pan with the rest of the butter and season to taste.

To make the mash, cook the potatoes in boiling water for 15 minutes, until tender. Heat the vanilla pod, cream and butter in a pan until the butter has melted. Remove the vanilla pod, and add the cream mixture to the potatoes and mash until smooth.

Deep-fry a few sprigs of parsley, stalks included, until crisp.

To serve, divide the mash between 6 plates and smooth the top and sides. Arrange the ceps and artichokes around the mash. Slice each chicken breast into 3 pieces and place on top of the mash. Spoon the sauce around and garnish with the fried parsley.

panna cotta with spiced oranges

serves 6

6 oranges and zest of 2 oranges

1 vanilla pod, split lengthways

165g (5½oz) caster sugar

900ml (1½ pints) double cream

5 tablespoons milk

3 leaves of gelatine, soaked in cold water

4 tablespoons vodka or grappa

1 cinnamon stick

1 teaspoon allspice

5 tablespoons water

fresh redcurrants and mint, to decorate

for the sugar spirals

150g (5oz) caster sugar

3 tablespoons water

Place the orange zest, vanilla pod and 100g (3½oz) of the sugar in a saucepan. Add 600ml (1 pint) of the cream and bring to the boil, then reduce the heat and simmer until reduced by a third.

Place the milk in a separate pan and warm gently. Add the soaked gelatine and stir until dissolved. Add to the cream mixture, stir, and pass through a sieve, then leave to cool.

Lightly whip the remaining cream and fold into the cooling cream mixture with the vodka. Pour the mixture into 6 ramekins (or similar sized moulds) and refrigerate for 4 hours, until set.

Meanwhile, peel the oranges and place the peel in a pan. Remove the pith with a knife, segment the oranges, and add to the pan with the peel. Add the spices, water and remaining sugar and bring to the boil, then reduce the heat and gently simmer for 15 minutes, until the sauce becomes syrupy. Leave to cool.

To make the sugar spirals, heat the sugar and water in a pan over a low heat, stirring gently. When the sugar has dissolved, bring to the boil. Boil the sugar, without stirring, until it reaches the hard crack stage (146°C/295°F), then leave to cool, stirring, until the mixture become syrupy. Dip a fork into the mixture and lift out a small amount of the sugar syrup, then twirl it around the handle of a wooden spoon to make a sugar coil. Remove carefully and allow to cool. (Make these no more than an hour before serving because they can become soft.)

Remove the panna cotta from the fridge and, using the tip of a knife, cut around the edge to loosen. Tip out on to serving plates and spoon the oranges and syrup around the edge. Decorate with redcurrants, mint and arrange a sugar spiral on top, then serve.

antonedelmann

Anton Edelmann is Maître Chef Des Cuisines at London's famous Savoy Hotel, a position he has held since 1982. Prior to this Anton worked in many hotel brigades in both England and his native Germany. A regular on television in the UK as well as, more recently, on the New York Food Network, Anton has published many books including most recently a book entitled *Afternoon Tea at the Savoy*. Anton is a very busy chef, keen to promote the Savoy via promotions and consultancies. These have included working in Japan, New York and Switzerland. The Savoy has a brigade of 80 chefs which is recognised as one of the busiest and most creative in London.

anton edelmann

menu one

starter

asparagus crown with crab

fish course

grilled irish salmon on minted pea purée
with a red pepper jus

main course

roast guinea fowl with a pistachio stuffing

dessert

marinated summer fruits & their soufflé

cheese petits fours

chutney crunchies
cottage cheese tartlettes
goat's cheese crostini
brie tartlettes
brioche croûte with mango chutney & roquefort

McKee Barracks, Dublin

wines

white

Gewűrztraminer, Weingarten, Cave Vinicole de Ribeauvillé 1998, France

The beautifully named Weingarten vineyard has the typically poor soils of the region, which is perfect because vines that are forced to struggle gain the most flavour for their grapes. The spicy nature of the grape, and its high acidity provide a good contrast with the asparagus and crab in this dish.

Chablis, 1er Cru, Mont de Milieu, J. Moreau et Fils 1997, France

A very dry wine with a crisp acidity, from one of the most famous Premier Cru vineyards in Chablis. Medium-bodied and with all the attractive steely characteristics of the Chardonnay grape grown in the northerly Chablis region. It provides a superb foil for the fresh salmon, without competing with its delicate flavour.

red

Fleurie, Domaine de Prion, E. Loron et Fils 1997, France

A wine with typical summer fruit aromas and a lively, fresh, grapey palate from a family-owned domaine located in this the most famous of the Beaujolais villages. Fleurie produces the most feminine examples of the single village Beaujolais wines, yet with enough weight not to be overshadowed by the full-flavoured guinea fowl and pistachios.

dessert

Le Cadet de Sigalas, Sauternes 1995, France

This second wine of the Ch. Sigalas-Ribaud, a Premier Cru Classé estate, exhibits similar qualities as its more illustrious "big brother", but is made from grapes grown on younger vines. Smooth and full-flavoured with strong peachy fruit flavours with hints of butterscotch, and backed by a cleansing acidity, it is a great match for soft fruit.

asparagus crown with crab

100g (4oz) plum tomatoes, peeled, quartered and deseeded

salt and freshly ground black pepper

32 asparagus tips, about 7.5cm (3in) long, blanched

125g (4½oz) white crabmeat

20g (¾oz) mayonnaise

Tabasco, to taste

175g (6oz) tomatoes, peeled, deseeded and diced

175g (6oz) avocado, diced

4 chives, blanched

curly endive and rocket leaves, to garnish

for the sherry dressing

1 egg yolk

1 teaspoon Dijon mustard

15g (½oz) sugar

1 clove garlic, crushed

1½ tablespoons sherry

250ml (8fl oz) olive oil

for the balsamic vinaigrette

3 tablespoons olive oil

1 tablespoon balsamic vinegar

salt and freshly ground black pepper

First dry the plum tomatoes: preheat the oven to 120°C/250°F/ Gas Mark ½. Season the plum tomatoes, place directly on a rack in the oven and bake for about 2 hours, until they have dried and shrivelled.

Cut the asparagus tips in half lengthways and arrange them around the inside of 4 x 6cm (2½in) plastic rings so that they remain standing up.

Prepare the filling by gently mixing the crabmeat with the seasoning and mayonnaise. Taste and add a few drops of Tabasco, adjusting the seasoning, if necessary. Fold in the diced tomatoes and avocado, then place the mixture in the middle of the asparagus ring and smooth the top with a spoon. Slightly raise each plastic ring to expose the bottom of the asparagus and tie the blanched chives around the base.

To make the sherry dressing, combine the egg yolk, mustard, sugar and garlic, then whisk to combine. Whisk in the sherry and slowly add the oil to make a vinaigrette-type dressing.

To make the balsamic vinaigrette, whisk together the oil and balsamic vinegar and season.

Place the asparagus crowns on serving plates and remove each ring. Arrange the oven-dried tomatoes around the crown and spoon over a little balsamic vinaigrette. Lightly dress the curly endive and rocket leaves with the sherry dressing and arrange around the crown, to garnish.

antonedelmann

grilled irish salmon on minted pea purée with a red pepper jus

4 wild salmon fillets, skin removed, each about 100g (4oz)

1 tablespoon black peppercorns, crushed

1 red pepper, roasted, deseeded, peeled and cut into 12 diamond shapes, to garnish

salt and freshly ground black pepper

for the red pepper oil

2 red peppers, roasted, deseeded and peeled

250ml (8fl oz) olive oil

for the ratatouille

1 onion, diced

1 dessertspoon olive oil

1 aubergine, diced

1 courgette, diced

3 tomatoes, peeled, deseeded and diced

for the minted pea purée

1 dessertspoon oil

25g (1oz) onions, chopped

1 clove garlic, chopped

200ml (7fl oz) white wine

1 tablespoon cream

500g (1lb 2oz) frozen peas

1 teaspoon chopped fresh mint

salt and freshly ground black pepper

First make the minted pea purée: heat the oil in a saucepan, add the onions and sauté for 2 minutes until soft. Add the garlic and sauté for a further minute. Add the wine, bring to the boil, then reduce the heat and cook until it has reduced by half. Add the cream and cook the sauce until it reduces to a coating consistency. Mix in the peas and mint, heat through, then purée and adjust seasoning.

To make the red pepper oil, combine the roasted red pepper and oil in a liquidiser and blend until combined, then pass through a fine sieve. Set aside.

To make the ratatouille, sauté the onion in the oil until soft. Add the aubergine and courgette and cook until softened. Add the tomatoes, stir, and heat through, then season.

Preheat the oven to 180°C/350°F/Gas Mark 4. Press the crushed peppercorns into the salmon fillets and season. Sear the salmon on a griddle for 2 minutes on each side, turning once to give a criss-cross pattern. Transfer the salmon to a baking sheet and cook in the oven for 6 minutes.

Warm and season the minted pea purée. Spoon into the centre of 4 plates. Top with the salmon and spoon over the ratatouille. Drizzle the red pepper oil around the pea purée and garnish with the pepper diamonds.

antonedelmann

roast guinea fowl with a pistachio stuffing

4 Savoy cabbage leaves (outer leaves only)

melted butter, for brushing

salt and freshly ground black pepper

2 guinea fowl

1 tablespoon olive oil

100g (4oz) pig's caul fat, soaked in cold water for 2 hours

300g (10½oz) onion, celery, carrot and leek, roughly chopped

herb bundle, made from a sprig of fresh rosemary, thyme and 4 bay leaves

75g (3oz) tomato purée

200ml (7fl oz) red wine

500ml (17fl oz) chicken stock (see page 171)

25g (1oz) butter, cut into small pieces

for the pistachio mousse

100g (4oz) chicken meat

1 egg white

200ml (7fl oz) double cream

25g (1oz) pistachio nuts, finely chopped

for the pommes fondant

2 large potatoes, peeled, halved and cut into even-sized barrels

300ml (½ pint) chicken stock

2 cloves garlic, crushed

1 sprig of fresh thyme

15g (½oz) butter, melted

for the Bavarian cabbage

450g (1lb) Savoy cabbage, inner leaves only, core removed and finely shredded

40g (1½oz) streaky bacon, cut into julienne

10g (⅓oz) unsalted butter

150ml (¼ pint) double cream

First make the cabbage sails: using the 4 outer leaves of the Savoy cabbage, remove the stalk and cut each leaf into a large triangle shape. Blanch and refresh. Brush with butter and season. Dry in an oven preheated to 110°C/225°F/Gas Mark ¼ for about 2 hours, until crisp.

To make the pistachio mousse, put the chicken and egg white into a food processor, blend until combined, then pass through a sieve. Put the mixture into a bowl, placed over another bowl of ice, and beat in the cream. Stir in the pistachio nuts and season.

Remove the legs from the guinea fowl. Trim and remove the thigh bones and fill with the pistachio mousse. Roll up and wrap in the caul fat. Pan-fry the guinea fowl legs and breasts (still on the carcass) in the olive oil until browned, remove and set aside.

Add the onion, celery, carrot, leek and herb bundle to the pan and sauté until the vegetables have softened. Add the tomato purée and heat through. Next, add the red wine and cook until reduced. Stir in the chicken stock, and set aside.

To make the pommes fondant, put the potatoes in a small, ovenproof dish and half cover with the chicken stock, then add the garlic and thyme. Brush the tops of the potatoes with butter and cook in an oven preheated to 180°C/350°F/Gas Mark 4 for 40–50 minutes, until golden on the top and tender.

Meanwhile, place the browned guinea fowl legs in a roasting dish, cover with foil, and cook in the oven with the potatoes for 15 minutes. Add the guinea fowl breasts to the dish and roast for a further 15 minutes.

To prepare the Bavarian cabbage, blanch the leaves in boiling salted water for about 4 minutes, refresh and squeeze out any excess moisture. Blanch the streaky bacon for 30 seconds and refresh. Melt the butter and fry the bacon until crisp. Drain thoroughly. Heat the cream in a pan until reduced by half and add the cabbage and bacon. Warm gently. Season to taste. Spoon the cabbage onto the bottom of the plate, and place the pomme fondant at the top.

Slice the guinea fowl legs into 3. Remove the guinea fowl breasts from the carcasses and slice on an angle into 3 pieces. Lay a breast on the cabbage with the bone to the right. Arrange the legs on top. Stand the cabbage sails up in the centre of the plate.

Add the small knobs of butter to the sauce, season to taste and cook until enriched and glossy. Spoon the sauce around the guinea fowl and cabbage.

chicken stock

This basic stock should be strong in flavour. If it is too weak, strain, and boil again to reduce further. It can be frozen in convenient portions.

makes about 1.2 litres (2 pints)

1 chicken, about 1.2kg (2¾lb)

1 onion, coarsely chopped

1 carrot, coarsely chopped

1 stick of celery, coarsely chopped

½ teaspoon black peppercorns, crushed

1 bay leaf

sprig of fresh thyme

a few parsley stalks

salt

Cut off the chicken breasts and reserve them for another dish. Remove as much skin from the chicken as possible and discard it. Chop the chicken carcass, wings and leg portions into pieces and put them into a large saucepan. Cover with 1.75 (3 pints) water and bring slowly to simmering point, skimming often to remove any froth that forms. Simmer for 10 minutes.

Add the vegetables, peppercorns, herbs and a little salt. Continue to simmer gently for 1 hour. Increase the heat so the liquid is simmering a little more quickly, but not boiling, and cook for a further 1 hour.

Strain the stock and allow to cool completely. Remove any fat from the surface before using.

antonedelmann

marinated summer fruits & their soufflé

juice of 3 limes

3 tablespoons dry white wine

4 tablespoons Crème de Cassis

2 teaspoons chopped fresh mint

60g (2¼oz) icing sugar

400g (14oz) mixed summer fruit such as raspberries, strawberries, blackberries, wild strawberries, blueberries and loganberries, washed

fresh mint, to decorate

for the soufflé

melted butter, for brushing

caster sugar, for dusting

2 eggs, separated

300g (10½oz) quark

finely grated zest of 1 unwaxed lemon

5 teaspoons cornflour

2 tablespoons light rum

6 tablespoons icing sugar

1 egg white

Prepare the syrup by combining the lime juice, wine, Crème de Cassis, chopped mint and icing sugar in a bowl. Stir well, pour the mixture over the berries and refrigerate for about 1 hour.

Lightly brush 4 x 7.5cm (3in) diameter x 4cm (1½in) deep individual soufflé dishes with melted butter, dust with caster sugar and shake out the excess.

Preheat the oven to 220°C/425°F/ Gas Mark 7. Mix together 2 egg yolks, the quark, lemon zest, half of the cornflour, the rum and half of the icing sugar in a bowl.

In another large, clean bowl, whisk the 3 egg whites with the remaining cornflour and icing sugar until the mixture forms stiff peaks. Stir a spoonful of the whites into the quark mixture to loosen it, then gently fold in the remaining whites with a large metal spoon.

Divide the soufflé mixture between the 4 soufflé dishes. Place the dishes in a roasting pan and pour enough cold water into the pan to come halfway up the sides of the dishes. Bake in the oven for 15 minutes, or until the soufflés are well risen and golden.

Spoon the berries and marinade into 4 bowls, turn out the soufflés and place on top, decorate with mint and serve immediately.

cheese petits fours:

chutney crunchies

makes 5

5 slices of mini baguette

garlic butter, for spreading (page 178)

50g (2oz) goat's cheese

1½ tablespoons double cream

5 tiny sprigs of fresh chervil or parsley

for the apricot chutney

makes 900g (2lb)

900g (2lb) fresh apricots, halved and stoned

50g (2oz) onion, finely chopped

150g (5oz) sultanas

1 tablespoon ground allspice

1 teaspoon freshly grated ginger

1 clove garlic, crushed

250ml (8fl oz) white wine vinegar

salt

300g (10½oz) preserving or granulated sugar

To make the apricot chutney, place the apricots, onion, sultanas, allspice, ginger, garlic, vinegar and a sprinkling of salt in a large heavy-based saucepan. Bring to the boil, then reduce the heat, cover, and simmer for 40 minutes. Stir in the sugar and cook gently until the sugar has dissolved, then bring to the boil and boil uncovered, stirring frequently, for about 40 minutes, until the mixture has thickened and the liquid has been absorbed.

Transfer the chutney to clean, hot jars and cover with acid-proof paper. Leave to cool, then cover with a lid. Store in a cool place until required.

Spread the slices of baguette with garlic butter and toast both sides. Place a teaspoon of chutney on each piece of bread. Cut the cheese into 5 even-sized pieces and place on top of the chutney.

Place the cream in a saucepan and cook over a medium heat until reduced by half. Spoon a little over each croûte and brown quickly under a very hot grill. Garnish with chervil or parsley.

pictured on page 174

cottage cheese tartlettes

makes 5

100g (4oz) cottage cheese

1 spring onion, thinly sliced

sprig of fresh mint leaves chopped, plus extra to garnish

salt and freshly ground black pepper

5 ready-made canapé cups

Put the cottage cheese in a bowl and mix in the spring onion and mint. Season with salt and pepper and spoon into the canapé cups. Garnish each one with mint.

pictured on page 174

goat's cheese crostini

makes 5

1 Crottin de Chavignolles (goat's cheese), marinated in herb olive oil

1 egg, beaten

1 tablespoon each of poppy seeds and sesame seeds, mixed together

5 small slices French bread, about 1/2cm (1/4in) thick, toasted

butter, for spreading

rocket and frisee leaves, to garnish

Cut the cheese into 5 slices and dip them in the beaten egg, then turn in the mixed poppy and sesame seeds until lightly coated.

Place the slices in a frying pan and cook them on both sides until the sesame seeds become golden.

Spread the French bread slices (crostini) with butter and top each one with rocket and frisee leaves.

Arrange the warm goat's cheese slices on the crostini.

brie tartlettes

makes 5

50g (2oz) brie, rind removed, and sliced

5 ready-made canapé cups

cranberry sauce, to serve

sprigs of fresh dill, to garnish

Put the brie in the canapé cups and cook under a preheated hot grill until golden. Top each tartlet with a little cranberry sauce and garnish with dill.

cheese petits fours, shown clockwise from top left:

cottage cheese tartlettes (recipe page 173), goat's cheese crostini, chutney crunchies (recipe page 173), brioche croûte with mango chutney & roquefort, and brie tartlettes

brioche croûte with mango chutney & roquefort

makes 5

2 slices brioche

unsalted butter, for spreading

5 teaspoons mango chutney

50g (2oz) Roquefort, crumbled

5 toasted pine nuts

Stamp out 5 neat squares, about 2.5cm (1in), from the slices of brioche and toast lightly on both sides. Spread each slice with butter and mango chutney. Place the Roquefort on top of the chutney and garnish each one with a pine nut.

antonedelmann

5th anniversary
celebration master class

menu two

appetizer

canapés:

goat's cheese in a seed crust

gourmet delight

tuna tartare

scallop croûte with sauce vierge

starter

smoked hock & goose liver terrine

fish course

courgette flower filled with seafood

main course

roast fillet of beef with port-glazed shallots

dessert

peach melba & pineapple pot-pourri

Lords Cricket Ground, London

wines

white

Château du Seuil, Graves Blanc 1997, France

Rich, supple, yet vigorous white Bordeaux with a floral bouquet of citrus fruits and honey and a touch of vanilla from oak barrel ageing. The Semillon element of the blend provides a rich mouthfeel to the wine, mirroring the richness of the goose liver, while the fresh and herby nature of the Sauvignon Blanc constituent provides a contrast with the hock.

Clifford Bay, Reserve, Sauvignon Blanc, Villa Maria Estate 1999, New Zealand

The ultimate expression of the aromatic Sauvignon Blanc grape, from the Seddon vineyard in the Awatere Valley on the South Island. Intense berry fruit, balanced juicy acidity and an incredible concentration and release of flavours, make it a real winner when served alongside the wonderfully rich seafood mousse.

red

Casa La Joya Gran Reserva, Merlot, Colchagua Valley 1997, Chile

A deep-coloured, highly concentrated Merlot of superb quality from Chile. With the typically noticeable yet soft tannins and long, full-flavoured palate, Merlot is an ideal grape for pairing with beef. The fruity character will also complement the sweetness of the shallots.

dessert

Côteaux du Layon, Moulin Touchais, Vignobles Touchais 1984, France

A rich, luscious wine with a ripe, honeyed character and a long lingering finish from one of the top producers in the Loire Valley. The relatively high acidity of the wine and its delicate nature (being from the northerly upper Loire), make it a refreshing partner for the rich, sweet character of the peach and pineapple desserts.

antonedelmann

canapés:

goat's cheese in a seed crust

makes 12

3 Crottin de Chavignoles (or other goat's cheese)

200ml (7fl oz) olive oil

small sprig of fresh rosemary

small sprig of fresh lemon thyme

small sprig of fresh marjoram

1 clove garlic, sliced

1 egg, beaten

about 2 tablespoons each of poppy seeds and sesame seeds, mixed together

12 slices of baguette

corn salad (lamb's lettuce), to garnish

a little vinaigrette dressing

for the garlic butter

2 cloves garlic, peeled

100g (4oz) unsalted butter, softened

salt and freshly ground white pepper

First make the garlic butter: blanch the garlic cloves in boiling water. Drain and crush finely. Add the garlic to the butter and beat well until evenly combined. Season to taste and set aside.

Cut each cheese into 4 slices and marinate in the oil, herbs and garlic for at least 4 hours. (The cheese may be kept for several weeks in a sealed jar.) Remove the cheese from the oil and wipe with kitchen paper.

Dip each slice of cheese in the beaten egg, then turn in the seed mixture until lightly coated. Place on a lightly oiled baking tray and bake in an oven preheated to 220°C/425°F/Gas Mark 7 for 2 minutes.

Spread the slices of baguette with the garlic butter and toast lightly on both sides.

Moisten the corn salad with a little vinaigrette. Arrange 4 leaves of corn salad and a piece of cheese on each slice of toasted baguette. Serve warm.

gourmet delight

makes 10

150g (5oz) beef fillet, very finely chopped

1 egg yolk

2 teaspoons finely chopped onion

1 teaspoon chopped capers

1 teaspoon chopped gherkins

2 anchovy fillets, chopped

4 tablespoons freshly chopped parsley

paprika

few drops of Tabasco

1 teaspoon Worcestershire sauce

1 dessertspoon brandy

salt and freshly ground black pepper

3–4 slices white bread

2 tablespoons vegetable oil

25g (1oz) unsalted butter

10 quail's eggs, separated and yolks reserved

10 sprigs of fresh chervil

20g (3/4oz) caviar

Put the beef into a bowl, then add the egg yolk, onion, capers, gherkins, anchovies and a quarter of the parsley. Mix well and season to taste with paprika, Tabasco, Worcestershire sauce, brandy, salt and pepper.

Cut 10 x 5cm (2in) rounds from the bread. Heat the oil and butter in a frying pan and fry the bread in batches until crisp and golden.

Dip the edges of the bread in the remaining parsley until coated.

Divide the beef into 10 equal portions and arrange on top of a round of fried bread. Place a yolk on top of each portion.

Garnish with a sprig of chervil and a little caviar.

tuna tartare

makes 12

100g (4oz) fresh boneless tuna, cut into small cubes, about 5mm (1/4in)

4 chopped capers

1 spring onion, chopped

1/2 teaspoon Dijon mustard

1 teaspoon fresh coriander, chopped

few drops of tamari (rich soy sauce)

1 teaspoon soured cream

1/2 clove garlic, very finely chopped to a purée

1 teaspoon lemon juice

1 tablespoon olive oil

1 tomato, peeled and diced

1/2 avocado, peeled and diced

salt and freshly ground black pepper

12 slices of toasted mini baguette

Put the tuna into a bowl and add the capers, spring onion, mustard, coriander, tamari, soured cream, garlic, lemon juice and oil. Mix in the tomatoes and avocado and season with salt and pepper.

To serve, spoon a little of the mixture onto each baguette slice.

anton edelmann

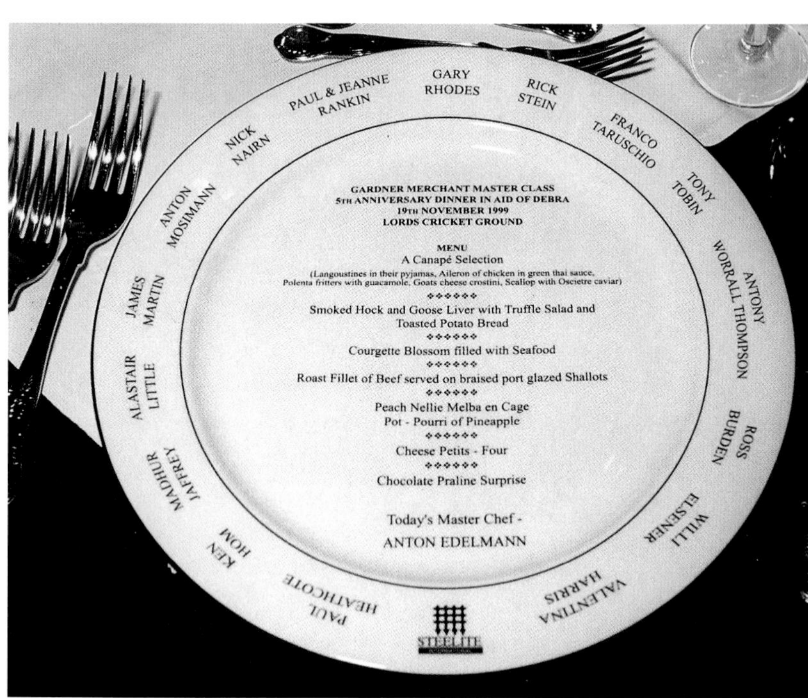

Fifth anniversary celebration Master Class plate

scallop croûte with sauce vierge

makes 10

10 thin slices of toasted mini baguette

25g (1oz) unsalted butter

15g ($\frac{1}{2}$oz) courgette, finely diced

20g ($\frac{3}{4}$oz) red pepper, blanched, peeled, and finely diced

15g ($\frac{1}{2}$oz) green sweet pepper, blanched, peeled, and finely diced

5 fresh scallops, cut in half crossways

2 tablespoons olive oil

for the sauce vierge

150ml ($\frac{1}{4}$ pint) sherry vinegar

2 tablespoons virgin olive oil

50g (2oz) plum tomatoes, blanched, peeled, deseeded and diced

1 dessertspoon each of chopped fresh parsley, dill, chives and chervil or basil

salt and freshly ground black pepper

First make the sauce vierge: mix all the ingredients together and season with salt and pepper. Leave for 1 hour to allow the flavours to infuse.

Meanwhile, spread the slices of toasted baguette with butter. Mix the courgette with the diced red and green peppers and place some on each slice of toasted baguette (croûte).

Dry the scallops on a kitchen paper and season generously with salt and pepper. Heat the oil in a frying pan and very briefly fry the scallops on both sides until just sealed.

To serve, place a scallop on top of each croûte and spoon a little sauce vierge on top.

smoked hock & goose liver terrine

serves 8–12

500g (1lb 2oz) hock

1 large onion

3 carrots

2 sticks of celery

2 bay leaves

10 black peppercorns

20 slices Parma ham

100g (4oz) goose liver, cut lengthways into 3cm (1¼in) slices

25g (1oz) parsley, chopped

100g (4oz) carrots, cut lengthways into 1cm (½in) pieces, boiled

salt and freshly ground black pepper

lettuce leaves, to garnish

1 tablespoon basil oil (see below) mixed with 1 tablespoon balsamic vinegar, to serve

for the white bean ragoût

500g (1lb 2oz) haricot beans

50ml (2fl oz) extra-virgin olive oil

150g (5oz) onion, finely chopped

5 cloves garlic, chopped

fresh thyme leaves

2 litres (3¼ pints) chicken stock

First prepare the hock: cover the hock with plenty of water in a large saucepan and leave to soak overnight. Drain, change the water, and bring to the boil. Add the onion, carrots, celery, bay leaves and black peppercorns and simmer for 4 hours or until the meat is beginning to come away from the bone. Remove the hock from the cooking liquor. When the hock is cool enough to handle, remove the skin, trim the fat and cut the meat into chunks.

To make the bean ragoût, soak the beans in plenty of cold water overnight. Heat the oil and sweat the onion and garlic, until softened, then add the thyme and beans. Add the stock and simmer for 1 hour, or until the beans are tender. Strain, reserving the bean mixture. Return the cooking liquor to the pan and cook until it has reduced and slightly thickened. Return the bean mixture to the pan, taste for seasoning and chill.

Line a 30cm (12in) terrine with cling film and then with the Parma ham, so the slices hang over the sides of the dish by 4cm (2 in).

Sear the goose liver in a hot pan for 5 seconds on each side. Season and place on kitchen paper. Allow to cool.

Mix the parsley with the cooked hock. Arrange the meat and the bean ragoût in alternate layers in the lined terrine dish. Then, in the centre, place the goose liver and surround it with the cooked carrots.

Fold the Parma ham over the top to cover and put a weight on top to press down the terrine. Chill for at least 3 hours.

Meanwhile, make the basil oil: blend a handful of fresh basil with 150ml (¼ pint) olive oil until puréed. Pass through a sieve.

Serve the terrine cut in slices, and garnished with lettuce leaves which have been dressed with the basil oil and balsamic vinegar dressing.

antonedelmann

courgette flower filled with seafood

4 courgette flowers, stamens removed, courgettes trimmed

250g (9oz) white crabmeat

3 tablespoons double cream

100g (3½oz) butter, melted

for the parsley and garlic sauce

2 cloves garlic, peeled

200ml (7fl oz) chicken stock

200ml (7fl oz) double cream

60g (2¼oz) fresh flat-leaf parsley, blanched for 30 seconds and refreshed on ice

for the saffron sauce

250ml (8fl oz) white wine

pinch of saffron

1 star anise

½ onion, chopped

120ml (4fl oz) double cream

120ml (4fl oz) fish stock

salt and freshly ground black pepper

for the seafood mousse

250g (9oz) white fish fillets such as sole, halibut, monkfish or brill, skinned

1 lobster body, blanched, shell removed

2 egg whites

400ml (14fl oz) double cream

cayenne pepper, to taste

To make the parsley and garlic sauce, place the garlic and chicken stock in a large saucepan and simmer until the garlic has softened. Add the cream and reduce to a sauce consistency. Add the parsley and liquidise.

To make the saffron sauce, put the white wine, saffron, star anise and onion in a saucepan and cook until reduced by two-thirds. Add the double cream and fish stock, and cook the sauce until reduced and slightly thickened. Season and liquidise.

Blanch the courgettes, without the flowers touching the water, in simmering salted water for 1 minute, refresh in cold water.

To make the seafood mousse, season the fish fillets and chill for 1 hour. Dry the fish with kitchen towels. Place in a blender and blend until smooth. Pass the fish through a sieve into a bowl, which has been placed over another bowl containing ice. Add 1 egg white gradually and mix in thoroughly. Add half the cream slowly and continue to mix slowly until incorporated. Season with cayenne, salt and pepper.

Blend the lobster meat in a food processor, then pass through a fine sieve. Put the lobster in a bowl, placed over another bowl containing ice. Beat the lobster meat until smooth but firm using a wooden spoon.

Gradually add the remaining egg white and beat until smooth. Leave to rest for at least 30 minutes. Gradually add the remaining cream to the lobster mixture. Add the fish mousse and season to taste.

Pipe the seafood mousse into the flowers, making sure they are full but no mousse is showing. Steam for approximately 5 minutes.

Meanwhile, heat the crabmeat with the double cream and season. Divide the crabmeat between 4 plates, place the courgette flowers on top at an angle and brush with melted butter. Spoon around the saffron sauce, then add droplets of the parsley sauce.

roast fillet of beef with port-glazed shallots

This is shown served on a bed of roasted new potato slices

serves 8

50g (2oz) butter

2 teaspoons olive oil

8 fillet steaks, each about 150g (5oz)

2 small fluted carrots, sliced

1 fluted courgette, sliced

1 tablespoon mild curry powder

salt and freshly ground black pepper

for the Port-glazed shallots

250g (9oz) small shallots, peeled

25g (1oz) butter

1 rounded tablespoon redcurrant jelly

150ml (1/4 pint) Port

for the basil sauce

3 tablespoons Dijon mustard

1 teaspoon balsamic vinegar

1 teaspoon sugar

salt and freshly ground black pepper

175ml (6fl oz) extra-virgin olive oil

50g (2oz) fresh basil, roughly chopped

3 rounded tablespoons roughly chopped fresh chervil or flat-leaf parsley

2 cloves garlic, chopped

1 rounded tablespoon pickled or salted capers, rinsed and dried

To make the basil sauce, place the Dijon mustard, balsamic vinegar, sugar, salt and pepper in a bowl and whisk in the olive oil. Place the mixture in a liquidiser and blend, then add the basil (stalks included), chervil or parsley, garlic and capers. Blend well and taste for seasoning, cover, and refrigerate until needed.

To make the Port-glazed shallots, blanch the shallots in boiling water for about 1 minute, then refresh under cold running water and pat dry. Melt the butter in a frying pan and add the shallots. Increase the heat to high and brown the shallots, turning them occasionally. Add the redcurrant jelly and Port, turn down the heat and cook for about 10 minutes, until the liquid has reduced and become syrupy and the shallots have softened. Season lightly with salt and pepper.

Meanwhile, preheat the oven to 200°C/400°F/Gas Mark 6. Heat a frying pan over a high heat until it starts to smoke, then add half the butter and oil and cook the steaks for about 1 minute on each side, until sealed and coloured.

Heat the remaining butter and olive oil in a frying pan, and sauté the carrots and courgettes for a few minutes. Season to taste and keep the vegetables warm while you finish cooking the steaks.

Remove the steaks from the pan and place in a roasting dish, then season well and sprinkle with the curry powder. Cook in the oven for 5–10 minutes, depending on how you like your beef. Remove from the oven and rest the meat for 5 minutes before serving with the basil sauce, shallots and vegetables.

peach melba en cage

2 large peaches

400ml (14fl oz) vanilla ice cream, to serve

natural yogurt, to decorate

for the sugar syrup

500g (1lb 2oz) caster sugar

1 litre (1¾ pints) water

50ml (2fl oz) lemon juice

for the raspberry sauce

300g (10½oz) raspberries

2 teaspoons lemon juice

40g (1½oz) icing sugar

for the tuile baskets

100g (4oz) plain flour

100g (4oz) icing sugar

100g (4oz) unsalted butter, melted

2 egg whites

for the sugar cages

250g (9oz) caster sugar

100ml (3½fl oz) water

10g (⅓oz) glucose

oil, for greasing

First make the sugar syrup: dissolve the sugar in the water in a pan. Add the lemon juice, bring to the boil, and cook until the mixture becomes syrupy. Leave to cool, then strain.

To prepare the tuile baskets, sift the flour and icing sugar into a mixing bowl. Quickly stir in the melted butter and egg whites to make a smooth paste. Refrigerate for 30 minutes. Place a star-shaped, eight-point cardboard stencil, about 13cm (5in) diameter, on a buttered and floured baking tray. Spread a little of the tuile mixture in the centre and draw a palette knife evenly over the surface. Remove the stencil and repeat to make 3 more stars. Bake in an oven preheated to 160°C/325°F/Gas Mark 3 for 5–6 minutes. While still warm, place the tuile over an upturned cup to form into a basket shape.

Poach the peaches in the sugar syrup for 1 minute, then peel. Leave to cool, then halve, remove the stones and set aside.

To make the sugar cages, mix together the sugar, water and glucose in a small saucepan and place over a high heat. Brush the sides of the pan frequently with a little water to prevent crystallisation. Cook the sugar to the hard crack stage (151°C/304°F). Leave to cool until the syrup thickens.

Lightly brush the outside of a 10cm (4in) diameter ladle with oil. Dip two dessert forks in the sugar syrup and flick very fine threads over the upturned ladle, changing direction to create a lattice effect. Turn the ladle on its side and finish with a thin line of sugar syrup around the edge of the ladle to form the base. When cool, carefully remove the cage from the ladle and keep in a cool place. Repeat to make 3 more cages.

To make the raspberry sauce, purée the raspberries in a liquidiser, then add the lemon juice and icing sugar. Pass through a fine sieve or muslin.

To serve, pour a little of the raspberry sauce on 4 serving plates. Place a tuile basket in the centre of each plate. Place a scoop of the vanilla ice cream in the centre of each basket and set a peach half on top. Spoon over a little raspberry sauce. Carefully arrange a sugar cage over the top of each tuile basket and place droplets of yogurt on the sauce.

pictured right:
Top, peach melba en cage, and bottom, pineapple pot-pourri (recipe page 188)

antonedelmann

pineapple pot-pourri

Pineapples are very reasonable and readily available, yet they are not often used as a pudding, which I think is a great oversight. Ripe pineapple has a flavour second to none. I created this recipe for a dining club called the Other Club, which was started by Churchill during the war and is now frequented by ex-prime ministers and senior politicians who invite the nation's opinion formers to dinner once a month.

1 pineapple, skin removed

300ml (½ pint) spicy stock syrup (see page 189)

8 egg yolks

240g (8½oz) sugar

300ml (½ pint) double cream, whipped to a soft peak

1 mango, peeled and cut into ½cm (¼in) dice

4 sprigs of fresh mint, to decorate

Cut from the pineapple 4 paper thin slices, reserving the remainder. Remove and discard the woody centre with a cutter and, using another cutter, cut the slices into 10cm (4in) rings. Dip the rings into the spicy syrup and place on greaseproof paper. Place in an oven preheated to 110°C/225°F/Gas Mark ¼ with the door open until dry and golden. Leave to cool – they should become brittle.

Cut some of the reserved pineapple into 4 x 1cm (½in) thick slices, reserving the remainder. Remove and discard the woody centre with a cutter and, using another cutter, cut the slices into 10cm (4in) diameter rings. Place the pineapple rings in a shallow ovenproof dish and pour 50ml/2fl oz syrup over them. Bake in an oven preheated to 190°C/375°F/Gas Mark 5 for 20 minutes.

Purée 50g (2oz) of the remaining pineapple in a liquidiser.

Whisk the egg yolks in a food processor. Meanwhile, bring the sugar and a little water to the boil in a saucepan until it reaches 120°C (250°F) and the sugar has dissolved and is syrupy.

Past Master Chefs enjoy the occasion

Add this sugar syrup to the yolks and whisk until cool. Remove from the machine and fold in the cream and the pineapple purée. Pipe into 4 x 4cm (1½in) deep x 7.5cm (3in) diameter ramekin dishes or moulds, smooth the top, then freeze.

Heat 200ml (7fl oz) of the spicy syrup. Add the mango and cook for 3 minutes, then allow to cool.

To serve, place the pineapple ring on a plate. Turn out the frozen parfait and set on top. Arrange the dried pineapple wafer on top and spoon the mango around it. Garnish with mint.

spicy stock syrup

makes 300ml/½ pint

300g (10½oz) caster sugar

2 vanilla pods, seeds scraped out

2 bananas, puréed

1 chilli, chopped

20g (¾oz) fresh ginger, chopped

50ml (2fl oz) dark rum

250ml (8fl oz) water

Combine all the ingredients in a saucepan, bring to the boil and cook until the contents are reduced by half. Allow to cool.

paul&jeanne rankin

The dynamic husband and wife team, Paul and Jeanne Rankin, have recently opened the fashionable restaurant Cayenne in Belfast. The name perfectly illustrates the dishes they create – spicy, vibrant and most of all fun. Since 1994, Paul and Jeanne have presented the BBC series *Gourmet Ireland*, showcasing the best of Irish produce and their own unique skills, and accompanied by two best-selling books. Paul and Jeanne are regulars on *Ready Steady Cook* as well as making numerous other television appearances.

paul&jeanne rankin

menu

soup course

spiced aubergine soup with cumin flatbread

fish course

seared salmon with asian coleslaw
& a soy-mustard vinaigrette

main course

peppered duck breast with wild mushroom
risotto cakes

dessert

catalan custard tart with a compote of oranges

Radbroke Hall, Cheshire

wines

white

Don Jacobo, Rioja Rosado, Bodegas Corral 1998, Spain

A delightfully deep-coloured rosé from Spain's premier wine region, with a fresh summer fruits nose and a zingy palate. Rosé wines with their light style, and generally lower acidity than white wines, make good partners for lightly roasted flavours, as found in this aubergine soup.

Antipodean White, Yalumba, Antipodean Wine Company 1998, Australia

An original Australian blend, incorporating the Sauvignon Blanc, Semillon and Verdelho grapes. It is a light, dry, aromatic white, with prominent tropical fruit flavours. The aromatic nature provides a good match with the spicy coleslaw, while the fresh, herby Sauvignon Blanc highlights the flavour of the salmon wonderfully.

red

Gnangara Shiraz, Evans & Tate 1996, Australia

A full-flavoured spicy Shiraz from Western Australia, with strong varietal character and soft ripe tannins. A great example of wine and food complementing each other: both have a peppery element to them, while the juicy, plummy fruit could have been produced with the duck in mind.

dessert

Côteaux du Layon, Moulin Touchais, Vignobles Touchais 1984, France

A rich, luscious wine, with a ripe honeyed character and a long lingering finish, from one of the top producers in the Loire Valley. The relatively light nature of the wine and its racy acidity contrast well with the light custard sauce, while the wine is sweet enough to cope with the caramelised sugar coating.

spiced aubergine soup with cumin flatbread

2 tablespoons vegetable oil

1 aubergine, peeled and cut into 1cm (½in) dice

1 tablespoon butter

1 large onion, finely chopped

2 cloves garlic, chopped

1 teaspoon chopped fresh ginger

1 teaspoon curry powder

1 teaspoon ground coriander seeds

1 teaspoon ground cumin seeds

1–3 serrano chillies, finely sliced

400ml (14fl oz) can coconut milk

600ml (1 pint) chicken stock

2 tablespoons Thai fish sauce

salt and freshly ground black pepper

4–6 tablespoons lime or lemon juice

3 tablespoons chopped fresh coriander

Heat a heavy-based, non-stick frying pan over a moderate heat. Add the oil and aubergine and fry for 10–15 minutes, until tender.

While the aubergine is cooking, melt the butter in a separate saucepan and add the onion, spices and chillies, then fry for about 5 minutes, until the onion has softened. Add the cooked aubergine, coconut milk, stock and fish sauce, then simmer for a further 5 minutes. Add salt and pepper to taste.

Stir in the lime juice and coriander and serve immediately with the cumin flatbread.

cumin flatbread

450g (1lb) fine semolina flour

400g (14oz) strong white flour

½ tablespoon salt

2 tablespoons cumin

1 tablespoon cracked black pepper

375ml (13fl oz) water

100ml (3½fl oz) extra-virgin olive oil

Sift both types of flour and salt into a large bowl and mix in the cumin and pepper. Combine the water and oil. Make a well in the flour and slowly incorporate the liquid. Knead to make a soft dough. Wrap in cling film and leave to rest for 30 minutes in the refrigerator.

Preheat the oven to 190°C/375°F/Gas Mark 5. Divide the dough into 4 pieces and roll out into thin sheets, about 3mm (⅛in) thick. Cut into long strips and bake for 5–8 minutes, until golden.

seared salmon with asian coleslaw & a soy-mustard vinaigrette

350g (12oz) boneless salmon fillet, skin removed and cut diagonally into 4

salt and white pepper

2 tablespoons vegetable oil

for the coleslaw

250g (9oz) white cabbage, finely shredded

1 small carrot, finely grated

2 tablespoons pickled ginger, finely chopped

3–4 tablespoons soy sauce, preferably Japanese

1 tablespoon peanut butter

1 tablespoon sugar

2 tablespoons lime juice

½ teaspoon chilli powder (optional)

4 tablespoons chopped fresh coriander

2 tablespoons finely sliced spring onions

for the crispy wonton

oil, for deep frying

1 packet wonton wrappers

for the dressing

2 tablespoons grain mustard

1 teaspoon English mustard

2 tablespoons caster sugar

2 tablespoons rice wine vinegar

2 tablespoons Japanese soy sauce

5 tablespoons vegetable oil

First make the coleslaw: in a ceramic bowl, combine the cabbage, carrot and ginger. In a separate bowl, mix together the soy sauce, peanut butter, sugar, lime juice and the chilli powder, if using. Add the cabbage mixture, and leave to marinate for at least an hour. Add the coriander and spring onions just before serving.

To make the crispy wonton, heat the oil in a wok or wide pan to 180°C (350°F). Separate the wonton wrappers and cut into fine strips, then deep-fry in batches until crisp and golden brown. Drain on kitchen towels, then sprinkle with plenty of salt and set aside.

To make the dressing, whisk together the grain mustard and English mustard with the sugar, rice wine vinegar and the soy sauce until the sugar has dissolved. Whisk in the oil to make a creamy dressing.

To cook the salmon, heat the oil in a large frying pan over a high heat. When the oil is very hot, add the salmon fillets, fry for 2–3 minutes on each side, and season to taste.

To serve, place a mound of the coleslaw at the back of 4 plates and top with a few crispy wonton strips. Arrange the salmon fillets in front of the coleslaw, and spoon the dressing around, then serve at once.

paul&jeannerankin

peppered duck breast with wild mushroom risotto cakes

4 female Barbary duck breasts

1 tablespoon black peppercorns, cracked

salt

50ml (2fl oz) cognac

200ml (7fl oz) duck stock, reduced to 100ml (3½fl oz)

100ml (3½fl oz) double cream

1½ tablespoons light olive oil

2 tablespoons butter

100g (4oz) shiitake mushrooms

100g (4oz) oyster mushrooms

25g (1oz) dried black trumpet mushrooms, soaked in hot water for 30 minutes, then drained

100g (4oz) fresh spinach, washed thoroughly

Trim the duck breasts and lightly score the skin with a sharp knife. Spread the cracked peppercorns over the duck breasts, pressing them into the skin. Season well with salt.

Heat a large pan over a moderate heat, and add the duck breasts, skin-side down. Cook for 5 minutes, or until the skin is nicely golden and crisp. Turn the breasts over and cook for about 4 minutes. Remove the duck breasts from the pan, and keep them warm while you make the sauce.

Pour off the fat, and deglaze the pan with the cognac, stirring well to scrape up the caramelised juices. Add the reduced duck stock and stir, then add the cream and simmer until reduced to a sauce consistency.

Heat the oil and half the butter in a pan and fry the mushrooms. Cook the spinach in the remaining butter. Mix the mushrooms and spinach together.

To serve, place a wild mushroom risotto cake (recipe page 200) on each warmed serving plate. Spoon the spinach and mushroom mixture over and around the cakes. Slice each duck breast diagonally and arrange on top of the risotto cake, then spoon around the cognac sauce.

paul&jeannerankin

wild mushroom risotto cakes

50g (2oz) butter

1 onion, finely chopped

15g (1/2oz) dried porcini, soaked in 200ml (7fl oz) hot water for 30 minutes

400ml (14fl oz) chicken stock

150g (5oz) arborio (risotto) rice

100g (4oz) brown cap mushrooms, finely sliced

salt and freshly ground black pepper

25g (1oz) Parmesan, freshly grated

3 tablespoons chopped fresh parsley

flour, for dusting

light olive oil and butter, for frying

Melt half of the butter in a heavy-based saucepan, add the onion and sweat for 5 minutes, until softened. Coarsely chop the porcini and add the soaking liquid to the stock.

When the onion has softened, add the rice to the pan and cook for a further 2–3 minutes. Add the porcini and the brown cap mushrooms, and cook for 2–3 minutes, stirring frequently.

Meanwhile, heat the chicken stock until simmering. Add 2 ladles of the stock to the rice mixture. Adjust the heat to a simmer and stir frequently. When the rice is almost dry, add another ladle of stock. Continue to add the stock, waiting until it has been absorbed by the rice before adding more.

When the rice is tender and creamy, stir in the remaining butter, Parmesan and parsley and season to taste. Turn out onto a baking tray and leave to cool.

Divide the rice into 4 portions and roll each one into a ball. Dust the balls with the flour, and then press into neat patties.

Fry the patties in a mixture of olive oil and butter, until golden on both sides. Drain on kitchen towels before serving.

catalan custard tart with a compote of oranges

serves 8

1 quantity sweet shortcrust pastry (recipe page 202)

1 egg beaten, to glaze

50g (2oz) granulated brown sugar

for the candied orange peel

100g (4oz) sugar

peel of 2 oranges, cut into fine strips

for the filling

750ml (1 1/4 pints) whipping cream

1/2 orange

1/2 lemon

1 tablespoon fennel seeds

1/2 vanilla pod, split lengthways

125g (4 1/2oz) sugar

9 egg yolks

compote of oranges, to serve (recipe page 202)

First make the candied orange peel: dissolve the sugar in 150ml (1/4 pint) water and cook over a high heat, without stirring, to make a syrup. Add the orange strips and cook over a low heat for 45 minutes. Strain the peel, then place on a tray that has been lined with greaseproof paper. Leave to cool.

Prepare the sweet shortcrust pastry. Roll out the pastry to a thickness of 5mm (1/4in) and use to line a 23cm (9in) flan ring. Chill for at least 30 minutes before lining with baking foil and beans.

Bake the pastry case in an oven preheated to 180°C/350°F/ Gas Mark 4 for 12–15 minutes, until golden, then remove the foil and beans. Bake for a further 1–2 minutes to allow any moisture to evaporate. Remove from the oven, brush the pastry with the egg to seal it and leave to cool.

To make the filling, place the cream and flavourings in a pan. Bring to the boil, remove from the heat, and leave to infuse for at least 30 minutes. In a bowl, whisk together the sugar and egg yolks. Strain the warm cream mixture into the bowl, whisking continuously to form a custard.

Reduce the oven to 150°C/300°F/ Gas Mark 2. Pour the custard into the pastry base and bake for about 30 minutes – remove when the centre is still slightly wobbly, like a crème brûlée. Leave to cool to room temperature.

Protect the pastry with foil to prevent it burning and sprinkle the top with the brown sugar. Caramelise under a hot grill or using a blowtorch.

Cut the custard tart into wedges and serve with the compote of oranges, and decorate with the candied orange peel.

pictured on page 203

sweet shortcrust pastry

150g (5oz) unsalted butter
100g (4oz) caster sugar
40g (1 1/2oz) icing sugar sifted
375g (13oz) soft flour, sifted
pinch of salt, sifted
2 egg yolks
1 egg
2 tablespoons cream

Place the butter, sugars, flour and salt in a food processor (or mixer with the K-beater attachment). Pulse until it resembles breadcrumbs.

Add the egg yolks, whole egg and cream and pulse again until it just comes together (do not overmix or the pastry will be tough). Turn out onto a clean work surface and pat together into a pattie-shaped disc. Cover with cling film and allow to rest in the refrigerator for 45–60 minutes before using.

compote of oranges

3 tablespoons water
200g (7oz) sugar
300ml (1/2 pint) orange (or mandarin) juice, freshly squeezed and strained
5 1/2 teaspoons cornstarch
50ml (2fl oz) Cointreau (or other orange liqueur)
4–6 oranges, peeled and segmented

Place the water and sugar in a small saucepan and boil over a high heat until it is a light golden, caramel colour (remember to have a glass of water and a pastry brush at hand to wipe down the sides of the pan).

Remove from the heat and add two-thirds of the orange juice. Return to a low heat and cook until reduced by about half.

Meanwhile, dissolve the cornstarch in a small amount of water and then add it to the orange juice mixture. Cook for a further 5 minutes.

Remove the mixture from the heat, and strain through a fine meshed sieve. Allow to cool slightly, and add the rest of the orange juice and the liqueur. Allow to cool – the sauce will thicken as it cools.

Marinate the orange segments in the sauce for at least 20 minutes before serving with the tart.

pictured right:
catalan custard tart (recipe page 201) with a compote of oranges

cyrustodiwala

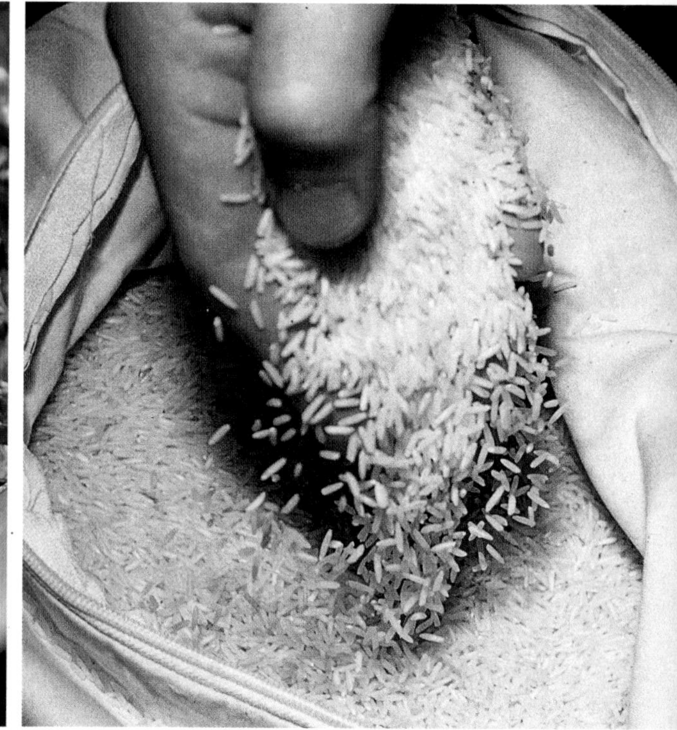

Cyrus Todiwala is the chef and co-owner of two Café Spice Namaste restaurants in the City of London and at Battersea. Cyrus trained as a chef with the famous Taj Group in India and subsequently worked in numerous restaurants, including the Geneva Inter-Continental in Switzerland where he developed French cuisine, enabling him to bring both French and Indian cultures together. He is a pioneer of 'new wave' Indian cuisine, always inventive and challenging. A visit to Café Spice is a must for visitors to London.

cyrustodiwala

menu

appetizers

a plate of starters:

sheek kabab (minced lamb with spices)

murghi na pattice (spiced chicken and potato cakes)

duck tikka (duck in tandoori spices)

kanda bhajia (onion bhajia)

served with tamarind and date chutney, yoghurt and salad

main course

ullathiyad (king prawn & scallops with fresh coconut, cumin & vegetables)

channa pulao (chickpea spiced rice)

dessert

lagan nu custard ("Wedding Custard")

Hampden Park, Glasgow

wines

white

Pinot Blanc, Les Ecumes, Cave Vinicole de Ribeauvillé 1998, France

This close relative of the Chardonnay grape, widely used in Alsace, produces an elegant, delicately flavoured wine with a refreshing appley palate and citrus finish. When choosing a wine to go with a range of dishes, it is wise to stick with light, neutral flavours; this wine will partner the duck and chicken well and provide a cleansing contrast with the rich sheek kebab and oily onion bhaji.

Estancia Chardonnay, Pinnacles, Monterey 1998, USA

An excellent Chardonnay, from the cool vineyard area of Monterey, with an intense ripe buttery fruit character and spicy creamy finish from barrel maturation. Both the wine and scallop dish have strong, creamy flavours, and the spicy aspect of the wine goes extremely well with the cumin and coconut in the sauce.

dessert

Forster Schnepfenlung Ortega Beerenauslese, Pfalz 1996, Germany

A luscious, very sweet, peach and apricot-flavoured wine with a lovely balanced acidity, which prevents the wine cloying on the palate. It is important to make sure that the wine is at least as sweet as the dish to prevent it from being overwhelmed. This wine copes well with the rich, sweet custard and adds complementary flavours to the dish.

cyrustodiwala

a plate of starters:

sheek kabab

makes 8

One of the many great representatives of Indian cuisine, sheek kabab or kavab is a street speciality. A Muslim dish, which can be traced to its Persian roots, sheek kabab also varies from state to state and region to region. This one appeals to most palates and to my understanding is one of the simplest and best.

Thick, square skewers are best but if you are not familiar with them use rounded ones. The skewers need to be thick, as thin skewers cannot hold the weight of the mince.

500g (1lb 2oz) lamb shoulder meat, sinew and gristle removed, and cut into small pieces (do not discard any fat)

20g (3/4oz) fresh coriander (including stalks)

20g (3/4oz) fresh mint (including stalks)

2.5cm (1in) piece of fresh ginger, coarsely cut

1 large fresh green chilli

6–8 cloves garlic, chopped

1 teaspoon garam masala

1 teaspoon ground cumin

1 teaspoon ground coriander

1/2 teaspoon ground red chilli

1/2 teaspoon turmeric powder

1 teaspoon lime juice

salt, to taste

Mince the lamb, coriander, mint, ginger, green chilli and garlic together. Add the ground spices and lime juice and knead well. Season with salt. (To check the seasoning, if you do not like tasting raw meat, either deep-fry a small ball of the mince or pan-fry a small patty-sized piece.) Cover the mince and chill.

Take a 5cm (2in) ball of mince in one hand and a thick square or round skewer in the other. Make the mince as smooth as possible by tossing it like a ball in your hand. Press the ball into roughly the middle of the skewer and press it around so that the mince covers that part of the skewer.

Apply a little oil or water to your palm and gently press the meat to form it into a sausage shape on the skewer. This does take a bit of practice; however, if you form a ring between your forefinger and the thumb and use the rest of the fingers to guide the mince you will be fine. The pressure has to be gently applied and the mince pushed upwards so that it spreads itself over the skewer. Ideally the size of the sausage should be around 2.5cm (1in) or slightly less in diameter.

Suspend the skewer over a small tray and repeat the process to make 7 more kebabs.

Grill or barbecue the kebabs, turning them occasionally, until done, but take care not to overcook them as this makes them dry and chewy. The kebabs should ideally feel spongy and should also show signs of a liquid presence inside.

Serve with a fresh green chutney and an onion-based salad, or roll in a chappati or a flour tortilla filled with salad and sliced onion and serve warm.

pictured on page 210

murghi na pattice

makes 20–30

This is a Parsee-inspired method of stuffing potato cakes. Both the Parsees and the Goans make several different types of pattice, and the "cakes" make excellent accompaniments to various dishes.

2 large or 450g (1lb) potatoes (use floury, old ones), sliced

1–2 tablespoons sunflower oil, plus extra for deep-frying

1/2 teaspoon cumin seeds

1 onion, finely chopped

2.5cm (1in) piece of fresh root ginger, peeled and finely chopped

3–4 cloves garlic, crushed

1 green chilli, finely chopped

250–300g (9–10 1/2 oz) chicken mince

salt, to taste

1/4 teaspoon turmeric powder

1 heaped tablespoon chopped fresh coriander

1 heaped tablespoon chopped fresh mint

2–3 eggs, as necessary

plain flour and breadcrumbs or medium-coarse semolina, for coating

Place the potatoes in a saucepan or a casserole and add just enough water to cover. Bring to the boil, then reduce the heat and simmer until tender. Drain and put the potatoes back in the pan and return to the heat.

Stir continuously with a flat wooden spoon or spatula, scraping the bottom until all the liquid has evaporated and the potatoes are fluffy and dry. Mash the potatoes or pass through a potato ricer. Place the mashed potatoes in a bowl and chill – do not cover if still warm.

Heat the oil in a frying pan until a thin haze forms over the oil. Add the cumin and, after about 30 seconds, the onion and cook until translucent, then add the ginger, garlic and chilli, cooking until the garlic becomes golden – do not allow the garlic to burn.

Add the chicken mince and turmeric and mix briskly, breaking up any lumps. If the mixture is very dry, preventing the chicken from breaking up, add a little water. Cook the mince until dry, then check for salt.

Transfer the mixture to a tray or plate to cool, then mix in the fresh coriander and mint, and taste again for seasoning.

Beat one egg at a time in a dish; place the flour and breadcrumbs in separate small trays.

Make equal-sized balls with the mashed potato. Take the potato ball in one hand and flatten it slightly, place a spoonful or less, depending on the size of the patty, of the mince mixture in the centre and fold the potato over the filling. Ensure that the potato completely covers the mince.

Form it into a ball and then flatten to form a smooth patty – do not make it too thin, for the casing will burst. Repeat until both mixtures are used up.

First dust the patties lightly with the flour, then dip them in the beaten egg and then in the crumbs or the semolina, whichever you prefer.

Heat enough oil to deep-fry the patties and fry until golden. Drain on kitchen towels. (Semolina will not brown as well as the breadcrumbs. However, it absorbs less oil and has a crisp texture.) Serve as a snack with chutney.

pictured on page 210

duck tikka

makes 20–30 pieces

Though duck is not commonly found on Indian menus, it does exist and is consumed in various forms in some regions. Wild duck is hunted during the migration period in northern India and in some parts of southern India.

This is a simple, yet delicious dish and one which is acceptable to most palates. It is ideal for barbecues or charcoal grills.

800g (1¾lb) duck breasts

1 heaped teaspoon turmeric powder

4 tablespoons lime or lemon juice

salt, to taste

100g (4oz) onions, coarsely chopped

40g (1½oz) piece of fresh ginger, coarsely chopped

40g (1½oz) cloves garlic, chopped

15g (½oz) red chilli, chopped, or red chilli powder

25g (1oz) ground cumin (jeera)

25g (1oz) ground coriander (dhania)

10–15g (⅓–½oz) garam masala

½ teaspoon black or white ground pepper

50g (2oz) tomato paste

200g (7oz) Greek-style yogurt

4 tablespoons sunflower oil

Remove the skin from the edges of the duck breasts but leave the skin down the middle. Cut the breasts into roughly 4cm (1½in) cubes and place them in a bowl.

Sprinkle half of the turmeric, half the lime juice, and some salt over the duck. Mix well with a wooden spoon to coat the duck and chill.

Purée the onions, ginger and garlic with the rest of the ingredients in a blender until they form a smooth paste. Combine the paste and duck pieces in a bowl, cover, and place in the refrigerator. Ideally the meat should stay overnight in the marinade, allowing it adequate time to penetrate and add flavour.

Preheat the grill to high. Put the duck pieces on a rack over a tray, so that the dripping juices can collect in the bottom. Grill until cooked but still a little pink.

Serve with a salad and fresh green chutney.

plate of starters shown clockwise, from top left:

sheek kebab (recipe page 208), kanda bhaji (recipe page 212), murghi na pattice (recipe page 209) and duck tikka

cyrustodiwala

kanda bhajia

makes 12–14

These are perhaps the most popular Indian snack in the UK and also the most misunderstood. The version available in shops and supermarkets does not even vaguely resemble the bhajia made in an Indian home. Try this recipe – it is very simple and the results will undoubtedly astound you.

2 onions, very finely sliced

2 green chillies, finely chopped

1/3 teaspoon chilli powder

2 tablespoons chopped fresh coriander

1 teaspoon cumin seeds, crushed

1/2 teaspoon ajawain (carom seeds, also called lovage), crushed

1/2 teaspoon lemon juice

6–7 tablespoons chickpea flour (besan)

1/2 teaspoon salt, or to taste

2 tablespoons water

oil, for deep-frying

Put the onions in a large bowl and add the green chillies, chilli powder, fresh coriander, cumin, ajawain and lemon juice.

Sift the chickpea flour with the salt, and gradually add it to the onion mixture, rubbing it in with your fingers until firm and sticky. Add the water and mix well.

Heat plenty of oil in a karai-type container or a deep saucepan but do not let it get too hot. Add small dollops of the mixture into the oil and fry – just a few at a time or they will become soggy. The bhajia should be no bigger than 2.5cm (1in) in diameter. Fry them slowly until crisp and golden on the outside and cooked through in the centre. If the oil is too hot they will be raw and gooey inside.

Drain in a sieve placed over a bowl and then serve immediately while still warm with a green chutney or tomato chutney.

pictured on page 210

ullathiyad

A delicious and very simple dish, which can be adapted to include various other foods such as chicken or a blend of various seafoods.

10–12 king scallops, halved horizontally

10–12 tiger prawns, shelled and deveined

1/2 teaspoon turmeric powder

1/2 teaspoon ground chilli

salt, to taste

1 teaspoon lemon juice

2 tablespoons sunflower oil

1/2 teaspoon mustard seeds

8–10 fresh curry leaves (use dried or frozen if you can't find fresh)

1 teaspoon cumin seeds

1 dessertspoon fresh, finely chopped ginger

5–6 cloves garlic, chopped

3 tablespoons grated coconut (if using desiccated select the fine-thread type and soak 2 tablespoons in half a cup of water for 30 minutes)

2 tomatoes, pulped and shredded with skin

8–10 mangetout, halved lengthways

1 carrot, cut into 2.5cm (1in) batons, or 8–10 baby carrots, halved lengthways, blanched

6–8 French beans or baby corn, halved or cut lengthways, if using corn

1 red pepper, shredded (optional)

4–5 spring onions, shredded

1–2 large green chillies, deseeded and shredded

1 1/2 tablespoons chopped fresh coriander

Place the seafood in a bowl and mix in the turmeric, ground chilli, salt and lemon juice. Stir well to coat and marinate in the refrigerator for up to 2 hours.

Heat a wok or frying pan until very hot. Keeping the heat high, add the oil and, as the oil begins to smoke, add the mustard seeds. When the seeds stop popping, add the curry leaves and cumin, then almost immediately add the ginger and garlic. Stir-fry for 1–2 minutes or until the garlic becomes golden – but do not allow it to brown.

Reduce the heat slightly and add the coconut. Sauté for a minute or two until the coconut emits a nutty aroma and becomes pale golden – do not allow it to brown.

Increase the heat to maximum, wait for a few seconds for the pan to heat up, but keep stirring. Toss in the tomatoes, mangetout, carrot and French beans or baby corn, then sauté for a minute or so. Add the seafood and, keeping the heat high, toss the pan from time to time. Do not agitate the pan too much or the seafood will release all its juices.

Add the red pepper, if using, the spring onions and green chillies and sauté for 1–2 minutes. Add the fresh coriander, stir, and check the seasoning.

Serve with the channa pulao (recipe page 217), or lemon rice or any other rice of your choice.

channa pulao

serves 6–8

Chickpeas come in various varieties. The most popular of all is the large white variety, also known as Bengali channa. High in protein, chickpeas can be used in several different ways. This is a simple pulao and makes an excellent accompaniment to many of India's great dishes.

425g (15oz) can chickpeas, drained, or 250g (9oz) dried chickpeas

3 tablespoons sunflower oil

2.5–5cm (1–2in) piece of cassia bark

3–6 cloves

1–2 large red chillies, halved

2 teaspoons cumin

5–6 cloves garlic, finely chopped

2 onions, halved and thinly sliced

500g (1lb 2oz) basmati rice

salt, to taste

onions, thinly sliced and deep-fried until crisp, to garnish (optional)

chopped fresh coriander, to garnish

If using dried chickpeas, cover them in water in a deep bowl or pan and leave overnight or a minimum of 6 hours. (The longer they are soaked the shorter the cooking time. However, prolonged soaking will ferment and spoil the chickpeas.)

Drain, rinse, and cover them in fresh water in a pan, then bring to the boil. Cook until softened, then drain and set aside.

Heat the oil in a deep pot or pan, with a tight-fitting lid. When the oil forms a haze, add the cassia bark, cloves and chilli. As soon as the cloves swell, add the cumin and sauté for a minute or so. Add the garlic, cook for 30 seconds, then add the onions and sauté until the garlic is almost on the point of browning.

Reduce the heat, then add the rice and salt. Stir well for 1–2 minutes. Add hot water or stock, covering the rice by about 2cm (¾in), and stir for a few seconds. Reduce the heat to a minimum and cook, covered, stirring every minute or so, until most of the water has been absorbed.

Add the chickpeas and cook over a low heat for 10 minutes, covered, stirring occasionally. Check the seasoning.

Serve the rice, sprinkled with the crispy onions and coriander.

cyrustodiwala

lagan nu custard

serves 4–6

A traditional Parsee-style baked custard and a must at festive dinners and weddings, hence its name, which translates as "Wedding Custard".

1 litre (1¾ pints) full-cream milk

150–200g (5–7oz) sugar, or to taste

4 eggs

1 tablespoon rosewater

½ teaspoon vanilla essence

½ teaspoon ground cardamom

½ teaspoon ground nutmeg

10–12 unskinned almonds, sliced

1 tablespoon charoli (this nut is available in Indian stores) and 10–12 unsalted pistachios, shredded or sliced, plus extra to decorate (optional)

Heat the milk in a large saucepan and bring to boiling point. Reduce the heat and simmer gently, stirring occasionally with a wooden spatula, for about 1½–2 hours, until the milk becomes a pale nutty brown and reduces by 30–40 per cent. Use a pastry brush and chilled water to keep the sides of the pan clean. Do this every few minutes but do not use a dripping brush, as it will dilute the milk. Do not allow the milk to burn on the bottom of the pan.

Add the sugar to the milk, stir, then allow to cool slightly. Pour a little of the milk into the beaten eggs in a bowl, whisking rapidly, then gradually whisk in the remaining milk. Taste and add more sugar, if desired, then add the rosewater, vanilla essence, cardamom and nutmeg. Pour the mixture into a large baking dish or individual dishes and sprinkle with the nuts.

Preheat the oven to 200°C/400°F/Gas Mark 6. Place the baking dish or dishes in a large tray, half-filled with hot water. This will prevent the custard from baking too rapidly, thus acquiring a broken texture when baked.

Bake for 10 minutes, reduce the heat to 180°C/350°F/Gas Mark 4 and bake until the top is golden. When cooked, insert the tip of a knife – it should come out clean. Leave to cool. Serve sprinkled with pistachio nuts (if using). Can also be served warm.

petergordon

Peter Gordon was born in New Zealand and has travelled extensively throughout Asia on a quest for food knowledge. Settling in London, he opened the celebrated Sugar Club restaurant in Notting Hill. Peter now concentrates his time on demonstrating his unique food style as well as organising yearly Leukaemia fund-raising dinners involving London's top chefs. He also contributes to numerous publications as diverse as the *Sunday Telegraph* and *New Zealand House and Garden.*

Peter has published two cookery books, *The Sugar Club Cook Book* and, in 1999, *Cook at Home*, and had a 13-part series on Pacific Food featured on the Carlton Food Network.

petergordon

menu

soup course

roast sweet potato, coconut & smoked paprika soup with goat's cheese wontons

fish course

grilled scallops with sweet chilli sauce & crème fraîche

main course

roast lamb chump on kale & roast garlic polenta with pea & mint salsa

dessert

poached tamarillo with honey yogurt bavarois & brandy snap

Cutlers Hall, Sheffield

wines

white

Barbadillo, Manzanilla de Sanlucar, Solera Pasada NV, Spain

This dry Manzanilla sherry is matured right by the sea and takes on an almost salty tang, which both contrasts and complements the different ingredients such as paprika, coconut and goat's cheese used in the soup: an excellent match.

Villa Maria Cellar Selection Chardonnay, Marlborough 1998, New Zealand

A blend of Chardonnays selected from three top vineyards and barrel matured with some barrel fermentation. The resulting wine is ripe, intensely flavoured with a creamy, toasty finish – a great foil for the sea-fresh scallops, creamy crème fraîche and chilli sauce.

red

Château Musar, G. Hochar 1993, Lebanon

Made in the Bekaa Valley from a blend of Cabernet Sauvignon, Cinsault and Syrah and aged for two years in French oak, this is an extremely full-bodied, ripe and spicy wine and an equal match for the roast lamb and garlic. The wine has a haunting sweet smell of mint and eucalyptus that also ties in well with the mint salsa.

dessert

Botrytis Semillon-Sauvignon Blanc, Yalumba 1997, Australia

A glorious golden dessert wine, produced from late picked bunches of botrytised Semillon and Sauvignon Blanc grapes, having a luscious balance of richness, sugar and acidity. The lovely peach and apricot flavours complement the honey bavarois, while the relatively light acidity of the wine contrasts with the more astringent tamarillo fruit.

petergordon

roast sweet potato, coconut & smoked paprika soup with goat's cheese wontons

300g (10½oz) orange-fleshed sweet potatoes, peeled and cut into 1cm (½in) dice

2 cloves garlic, peeled and halved

1 teaspoon fresh rosemary leaves

1 small thumb-sized piece of fresh ginger, peeled and grated

1 large red onion, thickly sliced

50ml (2fl oz) olive oil

½ cup desiccated coconut

1 heaped teaspoon sweet smoked paprika

300ml (½ pint) vegetable stock

200ml (7fl oz) coconut cream

2 tablespoons fish sauce

4 teaspoons lime juice

100g (4oz) fresh coconut, shelled and finely peeled using a potato peeler

2 teaspoons light sesame oil

½ teaspoon icing sugar

75g (3oz) goat's cheese, a sharp, moist type is preferable

3 spring onions, finely sliced

salt

4 wonton wrappers

1 egg, beaten

oil, for deep-frying

Preheat the oven to 180°C/350°F/Gas Mark 4. Place the sweet potatoes, garlic, rosemary, ginger, onion and olive oil in a ceramic roasting dish, then toss well. Roast the sweet potatoes for 30 minutes, stirring once, until they are tender. Cook them for longer if they are still hard. Sprinkle the desiccated coconut over the top and bake until golden, then mix it into the sweet potato mixture and cook for a further 5 minutes. Remove from the oven, and add the smoked paprika. Purée or blend the mixture until it is almost smooth but still retains traces of coconut.

Bring the stock and coconut cream to the boil in a saucepan, then add the purée, reduce to a simmer and season with the fish sauce and lime juice.

Meanwhile, toss the fresh coconut with the sesame oil and icing sugar and lay it on a non-stick baking sheet. Roast in an oven preheated to 160°C/325°F/Gas Mark 3 until golden and crisp. Leave to cool on a rack, then store in an airtight container.

Mix the goat's cheese with half the spring onions and a pinch of salt, and divide it into 4 balls. Place one ball in the centre of each wonton wrapper, brush with the egg wash and fold into whatever shape you want.

When the soup is almost ready, deep-fry the wontons until crisp. To serve, ladle the soup into 4 bowls, add a wonton, and garnish with coconut shavings and the remaining spring onions.

grilled scallops with sweet chilli sauce & crème fraîche

The sweet chilli sauce will make more than you need but it will keep for a month if stored in a jar in the fridge.

12 large, diver-caught scallops, trimmed

sesame oil, for brushing

salt and freshly ground black pepper

rocket leaves, to garnish

120ml (4fl oz) crème fraîche

for the sweet chilli sauce

10 cloves garlic, peeled

3 large red chillies, stems removed

3 thumb-sized pieces of fresh ginger, peeled and roughly chopped

1 thumb-sized piece of galangal, peeled and roughly chopped

8 fresh kaffir lime leaves

3 lemongrass stems, 2 outside leaves removed and centre finely chopped

1 bunch fresh coriander, stems and roots are fine, so long as your food processor is sharp

250g (9oz) caster sugar

85ml (3fl oz) cider vinegar

40ml (1¾fl oz) nam pla (Thai fish sauce)

40ml (1¾fl oz) tamari (soy sauce)

First make the sweet chilli sauce: put the first 7 ingredients in a food processor and blend until it forms a coarse paste.

Put the sugar into a saucepan with 4 tablespoons of water and place over a moderate heat. Stir well until the sugar has dissolved, then increase the heat to high and boil, without stirring, for about 5–8 minutes, until it has turned a dark caramel colour.

Stir in the paste and bring the sauce back to the boil, then add the cider vinegar, nam pla and tamari. Return the sauce to the boil and simmer for 1 minute. Leave to cool.

Brush the scallops with the sesame oil and season. Heat a griddle pan and chargrill for 45–60 seconds on each side, depending on size.

To serve, sit the scallops on a bed of rocket leaves, then drizzle the sweet chilli sauce over the top and place a dollop of crème fraîche in the middle.

...t lamb chump on kale & roast garlic polenta with pea & mint salsa

4 trimmed lamb chumps, each about 225g (8oz), fat "slashed"

2 teaspoons fresh oregano

salt

olive oil, for rubbing and frying

2 shallots, finely sliced

100g (4oz) trimmed kale, shredded and washed, still a little moist

50ml (2fl oz) light soy sauce

600ml (1 pint) brown chicken stock

150g (5oz) polenta, sieved

½ head of garlic, roasted whole in the oven for 35 minutes, then peeled and crushed

small handful of fresh basil leaves

freshly ground black pepper

for the salsa

150g (5oz) peas, fresh or frozen

small handful of fresh parsley

small handful of fresh mint

small handful of fresh coriander leaves

2 spring onions, finely sliced

85ml (3fl oz) rice wine vinegar

85ml (3fl oz) extra-virgin olive oil

Rub the oregano, some salt and a few teaspoons of olive oil into the lamb. Leave the lamb to rest for 20 minutes before cooking. Preheat the oven to 200°C/400°F/ Gas Mark 6.

Heat a frying pan and add the lamb, fat-side down – no extra oil is necessary. Cook over a high heat until the fat browns, turn over and brown on all sides, then turn again so that the lamb is fat-side down again.

Transfer the lamb to a large roasting tin and roast the lamb for 6–8 minutes in the oven, until done but still pink in the centre. Remove from the oven and leave to rest for 10 minutes.

Meanwhile, in a large saucepan, fry the shallots in a little olive oil until golden. Add the kale and sauté for 5 minutes, until tender. Remove from the pan. Set aside.

Add the soy sauce and stock to the pan and bring to the boil, reduce the heat and simmer. Gradually whisk in the polenta, allow it to simmer and bubble, then add the garlic, shallots, kale, basil and black pepper. Stir and simmer for a few more minutes, adding more boiling water if the mixture becomes too thick.

To make the salsa, cook the peas until just done, then drain and refresh under cold running water. Place the parsley, mint, coriander and spring onions in a food processor and roughly chop. Add three-quarters of the peas and blitz to a rough purée, add the vinegar and olive oil, blitz for 2 seconds and remove. Mix in the remaining peas, taste for seasoning and set aside.

To serve, spoon some of the polenta on the centre of a plate, slice the lamb against the grain and lay on top, not fanning it out too thinly, then place a dollop of the salsa on top.

poached tamarillo with honey yogurt bavarois & brandy snap

The brandy snaps can be made up to 5 days in advance and stored in an airtight container in a cool place. The bavarois will keep for 4 days in the fridge, as will the tamarillos.

serves 6

6 tamarillos, pointed end marked with an X

450ml (15fl oz) red wine

200g (7oz) unrefined caster sugar

2 star anise

1 small cinnamon stick

½ red chilli

for the brandy snaps

50g (2oz) golden syrup

50g (2oz) caster sugar

50g (2oz) unsalted butter

50g (2oz) plain flour, sifted

for the bavarois

500ml (18fl oz) double cream

1 vanilla pod, seeds scraped out

½ teaspoon finely grated orange zest

200ml (7fl oz) light honey

4 leaves of gelatine, soaked in cold water for 4 minutes

600ml (1 pint) Greek sheep's yogurt (cow's milk yogurt is fine for this, but I prefer the sharpness of the sheep's yogurt)

First make the brandy snaps: put the golden syrup, sugar and butter in a pan and boil, stirring continuously, until the mixture becomes light brown in colour. Remove from the heat and stir in the flour, making sure there are no lumps. Return to the heat and cook over a gentle heat, stirring continuously, for 30 seconds – it will colour a little in this time. Remove from the heat and leave the mixture to cool for 10 minutes.

Preheat the oven to 200°C/400°F/ Gas Mark 6. Take a marble-sized piece of the mixture in your hand, then place it on a baking tray lined with non-stick baking parchment, and flatten it out as thin as you can. These spread quite a lot so start with just 4 per tray. Place in the preheated oven and cook for 5–8 minutes. They are ready when they are a dark golden colour and quite bubbly. Remove the tray from the oven and let them cool slightly. When they are cool enough to handle, remove from the parchment and curl into a cone shape, letting them rest in coffee cups until set.

To make the bavarois, bring 150ml (¼ pint) of the double cream, the vanilla seeds, orange zest and honey to the boil in a saucepan. Remove from the heat and add the gelatine, stir until dissolved. Leave to cool but do not allow it to set, then strain the mixture to remove the orange zest. (If the mixture does set at this stage, carefully warm it over a pan of hot water, mixing well until it softens again.)

Whisk in the yogurt. Lightly whip the rest of the double cream, then gently fold it into the yogurt mixture. Pour it into 175ml (6fl oz) dariole moulds and leave to set in the fridge for about 4 hours.

To poach the tamarillos, bring the wine, sugar, star anise, cinnamon and chilli to the boil in a pan. Place the tamarillos in the boiling liquid, return to the boil, then reduce the heat. Cover the pan and simmer for 2 minutes. Leave to cool completely in the liquid.

Turn out the bavarois, top with a brandy snap and serve with a tamarillo and a little syrup.

inspiredchefs

This collection of diverse and creative recipes comes from Sodexho Chefs who have been inspired following their unique experience of working with each of our Master Chefs.

All serve 4

starters & light meals

home-smoked salmon with tartare, hollandaise sauce & oriental dressing

Debbie Kelly-Greaves – inspired by Tony Tobin

oriental lamb salad with thai dressing

Darren O'Neil – inspired by Peter Gordon

chargrilled squid with a spicy coriander salad

John Whybrew – inspired by Franco Taruschio

seared beef salad with spiced beetroot & blue cheese dressing

Peader Daly – inspired by Paul and Jeanne Rankin

smoked chicken with avocado salsa, herb salad & pepper "paint"

Peter Joyner – inspired by Nick Nairn

main courses

cod with roasted glazed beetroot & garlic

Steve Holder – inspired by Paul Heathcote

roast rack of lamb with aubergine caviar

Andrew Gernon – inspired by Gary Rhodes

thai-style halibut with egg noodles

Mark Rees – inspired by Ross Burden

seared calves liver with red cabbage & savoury puy lentils

David Scott – inspired by Antony Worrall Thompson

pork rice paper parcels with sweet & sour coleslaw

Paul Burton – inspired by Ken Hom

saffron-scented sea bass with warm beetroot & potato salad

Malcolm Emery – inspired by Alastair Little

chicken kebab "methi murgh"

Michael Dornan – inspired by Cyrus Todiwala

desserts

roasted pear with vanilla ice cream & a chilli froth

Fiona Sweeting – inspired by James Martin

exotic fruit with a champagne sorbet

Andrew Scott – inspired by Anton Edelmann

home-smoked salmon with tartare, hollandaise sauce & oriental dressing

350–450g (12oz–1lb) Scottish salmon fillet, skin removed and trimmed

salt and freshly ground black pepper

75g (3oz) cucumber, finely diced

juice and zest of 1 lemon

small bunch of fresh dill, chopped

1 bunch of fresh chives, chopped

250ml (8fl oz) olive oil, plus extra for brushing

2 slices brown bread, crusts removed

oak chips, for smoking

rocket leaves, to garnish

for the oriental dressing

120ml (4fl oz) soy sauce

1 clove garlic, crushed

thumb-sized piece of fresh ginger, finely chopped

50g (2oz) caster sugar

for the hollandaise sauce

1 tablespoon white wine vinegar

2 crushed peppercorns

2 egg yolks

225g (8oz) unsalted clarified butter, melted

Cut the salmon into 4 x 75g (3oz) fillets, then season and set aside. To prepare the tartare, dice the rest of the salmon and mix with the cucumber, lemon juice and zest, and dill. Season to taste. To make the chive oil, place the chives in a blender or liquidiser with the oil and blend until

home-smoked salmon with tartare, hollandaise sauce & oriental dressing

smooth, season and pass through a sieve. Set aside.

To prepare the oriental dressing, place the soy, garlic, ginger and sugar in a pan, and cook until it becomes syrupy and has reduced by half, then set aside.

Preheat the oven to 200°C/400°F/ Gas Mark 6. Roll out the slices of bread until they form an oblong and are very thin. Cut each slice in half diagonally and place on a baking sheet. Brush with olive oil and bake until crisp and golden. Season to taste. Drape over a rolling pin to curl, if desired. Allow to cool.

To make the hollandaise, place the vinegar and peppercorns in a pan and heat until the liquid has almost evaporated. Transfer the mixture to a bowl, then add the egg yolks and a dessertspoon of water. Place the bowl over a pan of simmering water and whisk until the eggs begin to thicken. Pour the butter into the egg mixture in a steady stream, whisking constantly until thickened. Keep warm.

Preheat the oven to 190°C/375°F/ Gas Mark 5. Heat the oak chips in a roasting tray over a direct heat until hot and smoking. Remove from the heat, then carefully arrange the salmon fillets on a rack which has been placed over the hot smoking oak chips. Cover with foil and bake for about 6 minutes, then remove from the oven and leave to stand to allow the flavours to infuse.

To serve, mound the tartare in the centre of each serving plate, top with the rocket leaves, then the salmon and crisp bread. Spoon around the hollandaise sauce and chive oil, then finish with the oriental dressing.

Debbie Kelly-Greaves (Craft Trainer, Kenley), inspired by Tony Tobin

oriental lamb salad with thai dressing

350g (12oz) lamb fillet, trimmed

50ml (2fl oz) olive oil

salt and freshly ground black pepper

salad and herb leaves, including curly endive, rocket, basil, chives and frisee, to serve

for the marinade

4 red chillies

8 spring onions, chopped

1 tablespoon finely grated fresh ginger

2 cloves garlic, chopped

8 tablespoons soy sauce

2 tablespoons white wine vinegar

juice of 1 lemon

3 teaspoons sugar

3 tablespoons chopped fresh coriander

for the dressing

juice of 1 lime

4 teaspoons white wine vinegar

2 tablespoons olive oil

First make the marinade: blend together the chilli, spring onions, ginger, garlic, soy sauce, vinegar, lemon juice, sugar and coriander. Spoon the marinade over the lamb and leave to marinate in the refrigerator for about 24 hours. Reserve the marinade.

Preheat the oven to 180°C/350°F/ Gas Mark 4. Heat a frying pan until almost smoking and seal the lamb. Place the lamb in a roasting dish and roast for 8 minutes. Remove from the oven and allow to rest before slicing.

Place the lamb marinade in a pan and cook until reduced by half. Pass through a fine sieve and reserve. Mix together the ingredients for the dressing and set aside.

To serve, slice the lamb and arrange in a neat circle in the centre of each serving plate. Pile the leaves on top of the meat and drizzle with the salad dressing. Spoon the reduced marinade around and over the meat.

Darren O'Neil (Tudor Hall School, Banbury), inspired by Peter Gordon

chargrilled squid with a spicy coriander salad

1 red pepper, deseeded

125g (4½oz) wild rocket

handful of fresh flat-leaf parsley and coriander leaves

12 baby plum or cherry tomatoes

1 tablespoon olive oil

8 new potatoes, boiled and refreshed

olive oil, for brushing griddle

4 medium-sized squid, tentacles separated and body cut in half lengthways

for the dressing

100g (4oz) red onion, finely chopped

1 dessertspoon finely grated lemon peel

50ml (2fl oz) lemon juice

½ cup chopped flat-leaf parsley and coriander

2 teaspoons sugar

2 small red chillies, finely chopped

2 cloves garlic, chopped

100ml (3½fl oz) extra-virgin olive oil

½ teaspoon hot paprika

First make the dressing: combine all the ingredients in a small bowl.

Preheat the grill to high. Grill the pepper, turning occasionally, until blackened all over, then peel and cut into strips. Mix together the rocket and herb leaves.

Preheat the oven to 160°C/325°F/Gas Mark 3. Coat the tomatoes in the olive oil and place on a baking tray; roast for approximately 40 minutes, until softened and concentrated in flavour. Meanwhile, slice the potatoes lengthways into 6 wedges.

Heat a griddle pan and brush with oil, add the squid and chargrill briefly until slightly blackened.

Toss the rocket, herbs, potatoes, tomatoes and pepper together in the dressing and arrange on serving plates. Top with the chargrilled squid, spoon over extra dressing and serve immediately.

John Whybrew (Food Services Development Chef), inspired by Franco Taruschio

seared beef salad with spiced beetroot & blue cheese dressing

2 tablespoons balsamic vinegar

350g (12oz) beef fillet, trimmed of fat and sinew

1 tablespoon olive oil

salt and freshly ground black pepper

salad leaves and herbs, to garnish

for the dressing

2 teaspoons Dijon mustard

3 teaspoons white wine vinegar

1 teaspoon lemon juice

100ml (3½fl oz) olive oil

50g (2oz) Cashel Blue cheese, crumbled

for the spiced beetroot

2 teaspoons salt

1 teaspoon each of chopped fresh oregano and thyme

1 teaspoon black pepper

1 teaspoon white pepper

1 teaspoon onion powder

1 teaspoon garlic powder

1 teaspoon paprika

1 teaspoon cayenne pepper

2 large beetroot, trimmed

2 teaspoons olive oil

chargrilled squid with a spicy coriander salad

To make the seasoning for the spiced beetroot, combine the salt, herbs, peppers, onion and garlic powders, paprika and cayenne in a dish. Put the beetroot in a saucepan of water containing 2 tablespoons of the seasoning and cook for 45–50 minutes, until tender. Reserve the cooking liquor. Run the beetroot under cold water and peel while still warm, then allow to cool.

When the beetroot has cooled, cut into 8 wedges and toss in 2 tablespoons of the seasoning. Heat the oil in a griddle pan. Sear the beetroot for 2–3 minutes, then place in a roasting dish in an oven preheated to 200°C/400°F/Gas Mark 6 for 10 minutes, or until dry. Meanwhile, reduce the reserved beetroot cooking liquor by half in a pan.

Set aside the beetroot and add the balsamic vinegar and 2 tablespoons of the reduced beetroot cooking liquor to the roasting dish. Simmer until reduced to a syrup.

To make the dressing, combine the mustard, vinegar and lemon juice. Slowly whisk in the oil until emulsified. Season to taste, then fold in the Cashel Blue cheese.

Cut the beef fillet in half, rub with the oil and season well. Sear the beef in a very hot pan for 2 minutes on each side, or longer if you prefer your meat well done. Rest the beef for 5 minutes, then cut into 12 slices.

To serve, arrange the beef and beetroot in the centre of each serving plate and top with the salad leaves. Drizzle the dressing over the top and spoon around the balsamic and beetroot syrup.

Peader Daly (Craigavon Area Hospital), inspired by Paul and Jeanne Rankin

smoked chicken with avocado salsa, herb salad & pepper "paint"

smoked chicken with avocado salsa, herb salad & pepper "paint"

2 charcoal barbecue briquettes

4 corn-fed chicken breasts, trimmed, each about 200g (7oz)

1 tablespoon vegetable oil

mixed herb and salad leaves, including rocket, chervil, frisee, mezuna and red chard, to garnish

1 tablespoon extra-virgin olive oil, to dress the leaves

for the salsa

1 ripe but firm avocado, peeled and chopped

1 red onion, finely chopped

1/4 cucumber, peeled, deseeded and chopped

200g (7oz) plum tomatoes, skinned and chopped

1 bunch of fresh coriander, roughly chopped

1 red chilli, deseeded and finely chopped

1 tablespoon Thai fish sauce

juice of 1 lime

salt and freshly ground black pepper

for the pepper "paint"

1 red pepper, deseeded and stalk removed

20g (3/4oz) caster sugar

50ml (2fl oz) white wine vinegar

1 yellow pepper, deseeded and stalk removed

for the balsamic reduction

100ml (3 1/2fl oz) balsamic vinegar

1 clove garlic, chopped

1 small piece of fresh ginger, roughly chopped

Mix the ingredients for the salsa together, and season to taste. Leave for at least an hour to allow the flavours to infuse.

Heat the charcoal briquettes in a roasting tray placed over a direct heat until red-hot. Arrange the chicken breasts on a large metal rack placed over the hot, smoking briquettes. Pour the vegetable oil over the chicken, then cover with foil. Leave the chicken to "smoke" for 20 minutes. Remove the chicken from the rack and set aside.

Place the red pepper in a food processor, add half the sugar and half the vinegar and about 50ml (2fl oz) of water. Blend until puréed, then strain through a fine sieve into a small pan. Gently reduce the mixture to a syrup, brushing the sides of the pan with a wet brush to prevent burning. Repeat the process with the yellow pepper.

Place the balsamic vinegar in a saucepan with the garlic and ginger and simmer until reduced to a syrup, strain and reserve.

Spoon the salsa into a ring mould and place in the centre of a serving plate, press down firmly and remove. Repeat until you have 4 servings.

Grill the chicken, then slice each breast and arrange in front of the salsa. Dress the leaves with the olive oil, season and pile on top of the salsa. Finally, spoon around the pepper "paints" and the balsamic syrup.

Peter Joyner (Senior Craft Trainer, Kenley), inspired by Nick Nairn

cod with roasted glazed beetroot & garlic

4 raw beetroot

20 cloves garlic, peeled

5 tablespoons olive oil

pinch of dried or fresh thyme

salt and freshly ground black pepper

750g (1¾lb) potatoes, such as Maris Piper, peeled and quartered

2 vanilla pods

100g (4oz) butter

4 cod fillets, each about 175g (6oz)

juice of 1 lemon

100g (4oz) shallots, finely chopped

200ml (7fl oz) double cream

500g (1lb 2oz) spinach, washed thoroughly

Boil the beetroot in salted water for 1 hour, until tender, then drain.

Preheat the oven to 180°C/350°F/Gas Mark 4. Slice the beetroot into wedges and place on a baking tray with the garlic cloves. Sprinkle with 2 tablespoons of the olive oil, the thyme and seasoning. Roast for 15–20 minutes, until the garlic is golden brown.

Meanwhile, boil the potatoes in a saucepan for 25 minutes, or until tender, then drain and mash.

Split the vanilla pods and scrape the seeds into the mash and add half the butter. Season and beat thoroughly until combined.

Season the cod with salt, pepper and lemon juice, then set aside.

Sauté the shallots in a little olive oil, until softened. Add the cream and the remaining butter, and cook until reduced by half. Fry the cod fillets in the remaining olive oil for 3–4 minutes on each side.

Sauté the spinach in 1 tablespoon of olive oil in a frying pan, until wilted, then season and reserve.

Pile the spinach in the centre of each serving plate and place the cod on top. Pipe a neat tower of mash behind the spinach. Spoon around the roasted garlic and beetroot and pour the shallot sauce over the top.

Steve Holder (Craft Trainer, Education), inspired by Paul Heathcote

roast rack of lamb with aubergine caviar

2 cloves garlic

2 sprigs of fresh rosemary, plus extra to garnish

600g (1 1/2lb) aubergines, halved and scored

120ml (4fl oz) olive oil, plus extra for frying potatoes

salt and freshly ground black pepper

2 large potatoes, peeled and cut into 3cm (1 1/4 in) slices

75g (3oz) unsalted butter

700ml (1 1/4 pints) lamb stock

1 rack of lamb (with 8 chops), trimmed

50ml (2fl oz) double cream

10 pitted black olives, diced, to garnish (optional)

To make the caviar, preheat the oven to 200°C/400°F/Gas Mark 6. Place the garlic and rosemary in the centre of each aubergine half, drizzle with half the olive oil and season. Put the aubergine halves back together, then wrap in foil and bake for 40 minutes, until soft and tender. Remove the aubergines from the oven and set aside to cool on a wire rack.

When the aubergines are cool, unwrap them and discard the garlic and rosemary. Scrape out the flesh into a bowl and chop finely, then cover and chill.

Make the pommes fondant. Use a 10cm (4in) diameter pastry cutter and cut the potatoes into 4 circles. Heat 25g (1oz) of the butter and 1 tablespoon of olive oil and sauté over a high heat until golden on both sides. Season to taste. Place the potatoes in a small roasting dish and cover with 200ml (7fl oz) of the lamb stock and bake in the oven until tender.

Reduce the oven to 180°C/350°F/ Gas Mark 4. Place the lamb in a roasting tin and brush with the remaining olive oil and season. Roast for 20 minutes, or until medium rare.

Just before the lamb is cooked, make the sauce. Put the remaining lamb stock in a pan and cook until reduced by two-thirds. Remove from the heat, add the cream and the rest of the butter, stir and strain.

To serve, reheat the aubergine caviar for 2–3 minutes in a small saucepan over a gentle heat. Arrange it in a diamond shape on each serving plate and top with the pommes fondant. Cut the lamb into 8 and place 2 chops on top of each potato. Pour the sauce around and garnish with diced olives, if using, and a sprig of rosemary, then serve.

Andrew Gernon (CGU), inspired by Gary Rhodes

roast rack of lamb with aubergine caviar

thai-style halibut with egg noodles

thai-style halibut with egg noodles

4 x 150g (5oz) halibut or turbot fillets or steaks

1 packet egg noodles

1 tablespoon sesame oil

½ bunch spring onions, shredded

2 carrots, finely shredded

100g (4oz) mixed peppers, finely shredded

fresh coriander leaves, to garnish

for the marinade

100g (4oz) onions, finely chopped

3 cloves garlic, crushed

25g (1oz) fresh ginger, peeled and grated

juice and zest of 1 lemon and 1 lime

4 tablespoons soy sauce

1 tablespoon ground coriander seeds

1 tablespoon soft brown sugar

1 tablespoon ground cumin

1 teaspoon chilli powder, or to taste

1 tablespoon olive oil

salt and freshly ground black pepper

Combine the ingredients for the marinade in a bowl and mix well. Lay the halibut in a non-metallic container and spoon the marinade over. Leave to marinate in the refrigerator for at least 3 hours but preferably overnight.

Cook the noodles in salted boiling water until tender. Meanwhile, warm the marinade in a small pan.

Heat the sesame oil, and add the onions, carrots and peppers. Cook briefly, then add the noodles and toss together.

Griddle or sear the halibut for 3 minutes on each side.

Arrange the noodles and halibut on the serving plate, garnish with coriander and spoon around the warm marinade.

Mark Rees (Oaken Holt Care Ltd), inspired by Ross Burden

seared calves liver with red cabbage & savoury puy lentils

100g (4oz) onions, sliced

1 tablespoon vegetable oil

100g (4oz) puy lentils

2 parsnips, chopped

2 baking potatoes, chopped

25g (1oz) single cream

100g (4oz) butter

2 glasses red wine

300ml (1/2 pint) beef stock

100g (4oz) smoked streaky bacon, cut into strips

25g (1oz) demerara sugar

375g (12oz) red cabbage, finely shredded

450g (1lb) calves liver

50g (2oz) flour, seasoned

salt and freshly ground black pepper

First make the onion crisps: preheat the oven to 180°C/350°F/ Gas Mark 4. Sauté the onions in the oil until browned, then place on a baking sheet in the oven until crisp and dry.

Put the lentils into a saucepan, cover with water and bring to the boil. Reduce the heat and simmer for 35–40 minutes, until tender. Drain and set side.

Boil the parsnip and potato until tender. Drain, mash and add the cream and 25g (1oz) of the butter. Season and keep warm.

To make the red wine sauce, pour the wine into a saucepan, bring to the boil and cook until reduced by three-quarters. Add the beef stock and cook for a further few minutes.

Sauté the bacon in a frying pan until browned and combine with the red wine sauce and lentils. Keep warm and set aside.

Heat the sugar with 25g (1oz) of the butter and 1 tablespoon of water in a pan. Add the cabbage and cook until al dente. Set aside and keep warm.

Dust the liver with a little seasoned flour and shake off the excess. Pan-fry in the remaining butter for 2 minutes on each side, until browned but still pink in the centre.

To serve, place the red cabbage on serving plates and top with the liver. Pipe the mash behind the cabbage. Spoon the lentils around the liver and top with the onion crisps.

David Scott (Chase Manhatten), inspired by Antony Worrall Thompson

pork rice paper parcels with sweet & sour coleslaw

pork rice paper parcels with sweet & sour coleslaw

600g (1 1/2lb) minced pork

30g (1 3/4oz) fresh ginger, peeled and finely chopped

1 bunch spring onions, white part only finely chopped

1 tablespoon sesame oil, plus extra for frying

2 tablespoons dark soy sauce

1 egg white

3 large cloves garlic, crushed

200g (7oz) basmati rice, cooked

50g (2oz) cooked petit pois

1 small bunch of fresh coriander, chopped

1 dessertspoon light soy sauce

4 rice paper wrappers

25g (1oz) flour

for the coleslaw

50g (2oz) carrot, finely grated

175g (6oz) white cabbage, finely shredded

2 dessertspoons clear honey

2 dessertspoons lemon juice

1 teaspoon chopped fresh ginger

1 tablespoon chopped fresh coriander

pinch of poppy seeds

First make the sweet and sour coleslaw: mix all the ingredients together and leave for 20 minutes to allow the flavours to infuse. Season to taste. Meanwhile, mix together the pork, ginger, spring onions, sesame oil, soy sauce, egg white and garlic in a bowl. Set aside.

Mix together the cooked rice, cooked petit pois, chopped coriander and light soy sauce in a separate bowl.

To assemble the parcels, briefly soak the rice papers in warm water until just pliable. Place them on a dry towel to remove any excess water. Carefully spread a quarter of the pork mixture over the rice paper, leaving a 5mm (¼in) gap around the edge. Spread over a quarter of the rice mixture and brush the edges of the paper with a little water paste to seal. Roll up the rice paper wrapper and tuck in the ends to make a spring roll. Repeat with the remaining rice papers.

Preheat the oven to 180°C/350°F/Gas Mark 4. Heat a non-stick frying pan, add the sesame oil and pan-fry the rolls until golden and crisp. Transfer to a non-stick baking tray and bake for about 10 minutes, or until the centre of the rolls have cooked.

Remove from the oven and leave to rest for 5 minutes. Cut each roll diagonally in half and serve with a mound of coleslaw, sprinkled with poppy seeds.

Paul Burton (Brands Product Development Manager), inspired by Ken Hom

saffron-scented sea bass with warm beetroot & potato salad

saffron-scented sea bass with warm beetroot & potato salad

1 sachet saffron powder

1 teaspoon turmeric powder

50g (2oz) flour

salt and freshly ground black pepper

4 fillets sea bass, each about 160g (5½oz)

50ml (2fl oz) olive oil

50g (2oz) clarified butter

150g (5oz) cooked beetroot (not pickled), cut into 1cm (½in) dice

150g (5oz) cooked potatoes, cut into 1cm (½in) dice

8 snipped chives

for the pepper oil

100g (4oz) roasted red pepper, deseeded and stalk removed

50ml (2fl oz) olive oil

for the coriander oil

1 large bunch of fresh coriander

6 tablespoons olive oil

First make the pepper oil: blend together the red pepper and olive oil until smooth. Season, then pass through a sieve. Set aside.

To make the coriander oil, blend the coriander and olive oil until smooth. Season, then pass through a sieve. Set aside.

Combine the saffron, turmeric, flour and seasoning on a plate, then dust the fish and shake off any excess. Pan-fry the sea bass in olive oil for 3 minutes on each side, until golden and the skin is crisp.

Heat the clarified butter in a pan and add the beetroot and potato and warm through, then season. Mix in the chives.

Arrange the beetroot and potato in the centre of 4 plates. Lay the sea bass on top. Drizzle around the red pepper and coriander oils.

Malcolm Emery (Sodexho Prestige), inspired by Alastair Little

chicken kebab "methi murgh"

- 8 boneless, skinless chicken thighs
- 200g (7oz) Greek yogurt
- 1 teaspoon lemon juice
- 1 teaspoon salt
- 50ml (2fl oz) ghee or oil, plus extra for brushing
- 8 cloves garlic, chopped
- 3 green chillies, finely chopped
- 5cm (2in) piece of fresh ginger, half chopped and half finely shredded
- 300g (10½oz) onions, finely chopped
- 1 teaspoon ground coriander
- 1 teaspoon chilli powder
- 200g (7oz) tomatoes, chopped
- 2 tablespoons chopped fresh coriander
- 125g (4½oz) fenugreek leaves

for the masala mix

- 6 cardamom pods
- 5 cloves garlic, chopped
- 2cm (¾in) cinnamon stick
- 1 bay leaf
- 1 teaspoon cumin
- 1 blade mace

Divide each thigh into 4 even-sized pieces. Mix the yogurt with the lemon juice and salt, then spoon the mixture over the chicken. Allow the chicken to marinate for an hour before threading onto 4 wooden skewers, that have been previously soaked in water.

Heat the ghee or oil in a pan large enough to accommodate the kebabs, and add the masala mix, stirring until the spices swell and just begin to colour.

Add the garlic, chillies and chopped ginger and fry briefly before adding the onions, coriander and chilli powder. Add the tomatoes and 4 tablespoons of water and stir to prevent the mixture burning. Continue to cook until the onions soften.

Pour the marinade from the chicken into the sauce and continue to simmer.

Meanwhile, heat a griddle, brush with oil, and add the kebabs.

When browned, remove the kebabs and place in the sauce to complete cooking. Add the shredded ginger, fresh coriander and fenugreek leaves and gently stir to combine. Cook for a further 5–10 minutes.

Arrange the kebabs on a plate and spoon the sauce over. Serve with warm Indian breads.

Michael Dornan (Head Chef, MOD Headquarters), inspired by Cyrus Todiwala

roasted pear with vanilla ice cream & a chilli froth

1 pear, thinly sliced on a mandolin

4 large pears, peeled and halved

450g (1lb) caster sugar

juice of 2 lemons

4 star anise

1 cinnamon stick

icing sugar, for dusting

25g (1oz) butter

25g (1oz) caster sugar

2 vanilla pods, split lengthways and seeds scraped out

100ml (3½fl oz) water

for the vanilla ice cream

250ml (8fl oz) double cream

250ml (8fl oz) milk

1 vanilla pod, split lengthways and seeds scraped out

6 egg yolks

100g (4oz) caster sugar

for the chilli froth

3 egg yolks

25g (1oz) caster sugar

120ml (4fl oz) poaching liquor

zest of 1 lemon

½ teaspoon finely chopped red chilli, or to taste

First make the ice cream: combine the cream and milk in a saucepan and add the vanilla pod and seeds to the liquid. Bring the mixture to the boil.

Meanwhile, whisk together the egg yolks and sugar. Pour the boiling milk mixture over the egg mixture, whisking constantly. Return the mixture to a clean pan and cook gently until thickened; do not allow to boil. Remove from the heat and strain into a clean container and allow to cool. When the mixture has cooled, churn in an ice cream machine, following the manufacturer's instructions.

To make the pear crisps, place the sliced pear on baking parchment and dust with icing sugar. Put into an oven preheated to 100°C/200°F/Gas Mark ¼ for about 2 hours, then allow the pear slices to cool and crisp.

Place the halved pears in a pan with the sugar, lemon juice, 2 star anise and cinnamon stick. Add sufficient water to cover the pears, then poach, covered, for 15 minutes, or until tender. Remove from the heat and allow to cool. Drain the pears, reserving the poaching liquor.

Melt the butter in a non-stick frying pan and gently cook the poached pears on each side until slightly golden. Add the sugar, vanilla seeds and remaining star anise and cook until the sugar has dissolved. Add the water and return to the boil and cook the sauce until reduced and a light caramel colour.

To make the chilli froth, place the egg yolks and sugar in a heatproof bowl, placed over a pan of hot water. Whisk until frothy, then add the poaching liquor. Continue to whisk the mixture until thickened, then add the lemon zest and chilli.

To serve, place the pears on 4 plates, spoon a little of the sauce over the top. Place a roundel of ice cream next to the pear and a dried pear on top. Spoon the froth around the pear.

Fiona Sweeting (Executive Development Chef, HSBC Group), inspired by James Martin

exotic fruit with a champagne sorbet

4 wafer thin slices pineapple, peeled

icing sugar, for dusting

for the champagne sorbet

300ml (1/2 pint) water

225g (8oz) sugar

300ml (1/2 pint) Champagne

for the exotic fruit compote

1/2 pineapple, peeled and cut into 1cm (1/2in) cubes

1 mango, peeled, stoned and cut into 1cm (1/2in) cubes

1 papaya, peeled, deseeded and cut into 1cm (1/2in) cubes

1 kiwi fruit, peeled and cut into 1cm (1/2in) cubes

1 sprig of fresh mint, leaves finely shredded

for the tuile biscuit

60g (2 1/4oz) unsalted butter

65g (2 1/2oz) icing sugar

2 egg whites

60g (2 1/4oz) plain flour

First make the Champagne sorbet: place the water and sugar in a saucepan and cook over a high heat until the mixture becomes syrupy. Allow to cool. Put the sugar syrup and Champagne into an ice cream maker and churn until sorbet consistency.

Dust the sliced pineapple with icing sugar and place on baking parchment. Put into an oven preheated to 100°C/200°F/ Gas Mark ¼ for about 2 hours, until crisp.

exotic fruit with a champagne sorbet

To make the exotic fruit compote, mix the cubed pineapple, mango, papaya and kiwi fruit with the mint. Spoon into 4 x 6cm (2½in) ring moulds and leave to firm for a few hours.

To make the tuile biscuits, place all the ingredients in a blender and mix to a paste. Line a baking sheet with baking parchment. Draw 4 x 8cm (3½in) circles on the paper and then spread a spoonful of the tuile mixture thinly over the circle, using it as a template. Bake until brown around the edges.

While still hot, lift the tuile off the baking sheet with a spatula and leave to cool on a wire rack.

To assemble the dish, place the compote in the centre of 4 plates and carefully remove the rings. Top with a tuile biscuit, the sorbet and pineapple crisp, then dust with icing sugar.

Andrew Scott (Catering Manager, Belmont School), inspired by Anton Edelmann

index

A minestrone of shellfish *144*, 145
Apple, prune & zabaglione tart 124, *125*
apples, Roasted nutmeg *110*, 111
Apricot chutney 173
apricot dip, Tunisian carrot rolls with 62, *63*
artichokes
  Artichoke & foie gras soup 14
  Frittedda (Braised spring vegetables) 36, *37*
  Jerusalem *see* Jerusalem artichokes
  Roast tournedos of lamb on seared artichoke filled with a cèpe duxelle *106*, 107–8
  Steamed guinea fowl with mash, artichokes, asparagus & yellow wine sauce 24, *25*
Asian coleslaw *196*, 197
asparagus
  Asparagus crown with crab *166*, 167
  Filo-wrapped asparagus & prosciutto 116
  Steamed guinea fowl with mash, artichokes, asparagus & yellow wine sauce 24, *25*
aubergines
  Ratatouille 168, *169*
  Roast rack of lamb with aubergine caviar 240–1, *241*
  Spiced aubergine soup with cumin flatbread 194
avocado
  Asparagus crown with crab *166*, 167
  Avocado salsa 142, *143*, 238–9, *238*

Ballotine of salmon on caramelised shallots, capers & black olives with a saffron water dressing 104, *105*
Balsamic dressing 14
Balsamic foie gras *63*, 65
Balsamic syrup 238–9, *238*
Balsamic vinaigrette 167
Basil sauce *184*, 185
Bavarian cabbage 170–1
bavarois, Honey yogurt *230*, 231
beans
  Green bean salad 84, *85*
  Roasted baby plum tomatoes & broad bean "stew" 147
  White bean ragoût 181
Béchamel sauce 33
beef
  Fillet of, with thyme, red wine & root vegetables *16*, 17
  Gourmet delight 179
  Roast fillet of, with port-glazed shallots *184*, 185
  Seared beef salad with spiced beetroot & blue cheese dressing 236–7
  Thai meatballs 90
beetroot
  Cod with roasted glazed beetroot & garlic 239
  Spiced 236–7
  Warm beetroot & potato salad 246–7, *246*
Blue cheese dressing 236–7
Brandy snaps *230*, 231
Brie tartlettes *174*, 175
Brioche croûte with mango chutney & Roquefort *174*, 175
broad bean "stew", Roasted baby plum tomatoes & 147
broccoli & baby corn, Hong-Kong style *96*, 98
burrata, Truffled, with roasted cherry tomatoes *63*, 65
butter, Garlic 123, 178

Cabbage
  Bavarian 170–1
  Chicken breast stuffed with porcini mushrooms *122*, 123
  Seared calves liver with red cabbage & savoury puy lentils 243
  see also coleslaw
cake, Chocolate, with candied ginger 99
calves liver, Seared, with red cabbage & savoury puy lentils 243
Canapés, Anton Edelmann's 178–80
Candied orange peel 201, *203*
Caramelised melba toast *110*, 111
Caramelised shallots 104, *105*
carrots
  Tunisian carrot rolls with apricot dip 62, *63*
  see also coleslaw
Catalan custard tart with a compote of oranges 201–2, *203*
ceps/cèpes
  Cep lentils 68, *69*
  Pan-fried, corn-fed breast of chicken with roasted ceps & Jerusalem artichokes 158, *159*
  Roast tournedos of lamb on seared artichoke filled with a cèpe duxelle *106*, 107–8
Champagne sorbet 250–1, *251*
Channa pulao (Chickpea spiced rice) 217
Chargrilled squid with a spicy coriander salad 236, *237*
cheese
  Blue cheese dressing 236–7
  Brie tartlettes *174*, 175
  Brioche croûte with mango chutney & Roquefort *174*, 175
  Cheese petits fours 173–5, *174*
  Cottage cheese tartlettes 173, *174*
  Marinated summer fruits & their soufflé 172
  Panzerotti fritti 32
  Spinach & ricotta risotto 120
  Truffled burrata with roasted cherry tomatoes *63*, 65
  Vegetable griddle cakes with soured cream & chives 61, *63*
  Vincisgrassi 33
  see also goat's cheese; mascarpone
chicken
  Chicken breast stuffed with porcini mushrooms *122*, 123
  Chicken kebab "methi murgh" 247
  Crispy, with ginger sauce 76
  Murghi na pattice (Spiced chicken & potato cakes) 209, *210*
  Pan-fried, corn-fed breast of chicken with roasted ceps & Jerusalem artichokes 158, *159*
  Prosciutto-wrapped chicken breast on cep lentils 68, *69*
  Smoked, with avocado salsa, herb salad & pepper "paint" 238–9, *238*
  stock 171
  Thai *96*, 97
  Thai barbecue *82*, 83
Chickpea spiced rice (Channa pulao) 217
Chilli froth 249
Chilli-garlic prawns 60, *63*
Chive oil 23, 131, 234–5
Chocolate cake with candied ginger 99
Chocolate tuiles *26*, 27
Chorizo oil *134*, 135
chutney, Apricot 173
Chutney crunchies 173, *174*
clafoutis, Raspberry, in a sweet pastry box with a lemon sabayon 136, *137*
Classic wonton soup *92*, 93
coconut/coconut milk
  Coconut tart with raspberry sauce, star anise ice cream & maraschino sabayon *52*, 53
  Roast sweet potato, coconut & smoked paprika soup with goat's cheese wontons 224, *225*
  Singapore curry crab 94, *95*
  Spiced aubergine soup with cumin flatbread 194
  Steamed fish with coconut *78*, *79*
  Sticky rice 132, *133*
  Thai-style steamed pumpkin custard 87
  Ullathiyad (King prawn & scallops with fresh coconut, cumin & vegetables) *214*, 215
coffee desserts, Trio of 38–41, *40*
coleslaw, Asian *196*, 197
coleslaw, Sweet & sour 244–5, *244*
Compote of oranges 202, *203*
confit, Fennel *134*, 135
Coriander oil 246–7, *246*
corn, Hong-Kong style broccoli & baby corn *96*, 98
Cottage cheese tartlettes 173, *174*
coulis, Raspberry 136, *137*
courgettes
  A minestrone of shellfish *144*, 145
  Courgette flower filled with seafood 182, *183*
  Ratatouille 168, *169*
  Vegetable griddle cakes with soured cream & chives 61, *63*
Crema bruciata di caffé (Coffee crème brûlée) 39, *40*
Crispy chicken with ginger sauce 76
Crispy shallots 46, *47*
Crispy wontons 77, *196*, 197

Crocchette d'eglesino affumicato con salsa d'aragosta (Smoked haddock fishcakes with lobster bisque sauce) *34*, 35
crostini, Goat's cheese *174*, 175
croûtes
  Brioche, with mango chutney & Roquefort *174*, 175
  Scallop, with sauce vierge 180
Cumin flatbread 194
custard, Lagan nu ("Wedding Custard") 218, *219*
custard, Thai-style steamed pumpkin 87
custard tart with a compote of oranges, Catalan 201–2, *203*

Dip, Apricot 62, *63*
dipping sauces *48*, 49, 77, 91
dressings 46, 157, 197, 236
  Balsamic 14
  Balsamic vinaigrette 167
  Blue cheese 236–7
  Lemon *130*, 131
  Oriental 234–5, *234*
  Saffron water 104, *105*
  Sherry 167
  Soy-mustard vinaigrette *196*, 197
  Thai 235
  Watercress 14
duck breasts with wild mushroom risotto cakes, Peppered 198–200, *199*
Duck tikka *210*, 211

Earl Grey syrup 149
eggs
  Gourmet delight 179
  Pad thai 50
  Seared salmon & poached egg with watercress dressing 14, *15*
  see also dishes made with eggs e.g. soufflés
elderflower omelette soufflé, Rhubarb & 18, *19*
Exotic fruit with a champagne sorbet 250–1, *251*

Fennel confit *134*, 135
Fillet of beef with thyme, red wine & root vegetables *16*, 17
Fillet of rabbit roasted in parma ham with fennel confit & chorizo oil *134*, 135
Filo-wrapped asparagus & prosciutto 116
fish
  Ballotine of salmon on caramelised shallots, capers & black olives with a saffron water dressing 104, *105*
  Cod with roasted glazed beetroot & garlic 239
  Courgette flower filled with seafood 182, *183*
  Crocchette d'eglesino affumicato con salsa d'aragosta (Smoked haddock fishcakes with lobster bisque sauce) *34*, 35
  Grilled Irish salmon on minted pea purée with a red pepper jus 168, *169*
  Home-smoked salmon with tartare, hollandaise sauce & oriental dressing 234–5, *234*
  Hot smoked salmon with avocado salsa 142, *143*
  Lasagne of marinated salmon with lemon dressing & chive oil *130*, 131
  Monkfish & mussels in spices 66, *67*
  Potted salmon with potato salad, soured cream & chive oil *22*, 23
  Saffron-scented sea bass with warm beetroot & potato salad 246–7, *246*
  Seared salmon & poached egg with watercress dressing 14, *15*
  Seared salmon with Asian coleslaw and a soy-mustard vinaigrette *196*, 197
  Seared salmon with rice vermicelli *156*, 157
  Skate & sweet spinach salad *63*, 64
  Steamed fish with coconut *78*, 79
  Steamed halibut steaks with garlic oil 50, *51*
  Thai fishcakes with dipping sauce *48*, 49
  Thai-style halibut with egg noodles 242–3, *242*
  Tuna tartare 179
flatbread, Cumin 194
foie gras
  Artichoke & foie gras soup 14
  Balsamic *63*, 65
  Yorkshire pudding with foie gras & onion gravy 154, *155*
Frittedda (Braised spring vegetables) 36, *37*
fruit
  Exotic, with a champagne sorbet 250–1, *251*
  Marinated summer fruits & their soufflé 172
  Pineapple pot-pourri *187*, 188–9
  see also by type e.g. apples

Garlic
  Cod with roasted glazed beetroot & garlic 239
  Garlic butter 123, 178
  Garlic oil 50
  Kale & roast garlic polenta 228, *229*
Gelato al caffé con salsa di caffé (Coffee ice cream with coffee sauce) *40*, 41
Ginger sauce 76
goat's cheese
  Chutney crunchies 173, *174*
  Goat's cheese crostini *174*, 175
  Goat's cheese in a seed crust 178
  Goat's cheese wontons 224, *225*
goose liver, Smoked hock & goose liver terrine 181
Gourmet delight 179
gravies 146, 154
Green bean salad 84, *85*
green onion pancakes, Shrimp & 60, *63*
griddle cakes, Vegetable, with soured cream & chives 61, *63*
Grilled Irish salmon on minted pea purée with a red pepper jus 168, *169*
Grilled scallops with sweet chilli sauce & crème fraîche *226*, 227
guinea fowl
  Roast, with a pistachio stuffing 170–1
  Steamed, with mash, artichokes, asparagus & yellow wine sauce 24, *25*

Ham *see* Parma ham/prosciutto
Herb oil 142
hock & goose liver terrine, Smoked 181
Hollandaise sauce 234–5, *234*
Home-smoked salmon with tartare, hollandaise sauce & oriental dressing 234–5, *234*
Honey yogurt bavarois *230*, 231
Hong-Kong style broccoli & baby corn *96*, 98
Hot & sweet scallops with sticky rice & crab chopsticks 132, *133*
Hot smoked salmon with avocado salsa 142, *143*

Ice creams
  Gelato al caffé con salsa di caffé (Coffee, with coffee sauce) *40*, 41
  Star anise *52*, 54
  Vanilla 249

Jerusalem artichokes, Pan-fried, corn-fed breast of chicken with roasted ceps & 158, *159*

Kale & roast garlic polenta 228, *229*
Kanda bhajia (Onion bhajia) *210*, 212
kangaroo fillet with crispy shallots, Salad of 46, *47*
kebabs
  Chicken kebab "methi murgh" 247
  Sheek kabab (Minced lamb with spices) 208, *210*

Lagan nu custard ("Wedding Custard") 218, *219*
lamb
  Oriental lamb salad with Thai dressing 235
  Roast lamb chump on kale & roast garlic polenta with pea & mint salsa 228, *229*
  Roast leg of, with garlic, rosemary, roasted baby plum tomatoes & broad bean "stew" 146–7
  Roast rack of, with aubergine caviar 240–1, *241*
  Roast tournedos of, on seared artichoke filled with a cèpe duxelle *106*, 107–8
  Sheek kabab (Minced, with spices) 208, *210*
Lasagne of marinated salmon with lemon dressing & chive oil *130*, 131
Lemon dressing *130*, 131
Lemon sabayon 136
lentils *see* puy lentils
liver, Seared calves, with red cabbage & savoury puy lentils 243
Lobster bisque sauce (Salsa d'aragosta) *34*, 35

Maraschino sabayon *52*, 54
Marinated summer fruits & their soufflé 172
mascarpone
  Mascarpone cream *70*, 71
  Panna cotta al caffé 38, *40*
meat *see* by type e.g. beef
meatballs, Thai 90
melba toast, Caramelised *110*, 111
minestrone of shellfish, A *144*, 145
Monkfish & mussels in spices 66, *67*
mousse, Pistachio 170
mousse, Seafood 182, *183*
Murghi na pattice (Spiced chicken & potato cakes) 209, *210*
mushrooms
  Peppered duck breasts with wild mushroom risotto cakes 198–200, *199*
  see also ceps/cèpes; porcini

Nam prik pla (Spicy dipping sauce) 77
noodles
Pad thai 50
Thai-style halibut with egg noodles 242–3, *242*
Vermicelli salad *156*, 157

Oils
Chive 23, 131, 234–5
Chorizo 135
Coriander 246–7
Garlic 50
Herb 142
Red pepper 142, 168, 246–7
omelette soufflé, Rhubarb & elderflower 18, *19*
Onion bhajia (Kanda bhajia) *210*, 212
Onion crisps 243
Onion gravy 154, *155*
Onion purée *16*, 17
oranges
Candied orange peel 201, *203*
Catalan custard tart with a compote of oranges 201–2, *203*
Spiced *160*, 161
Oriental dressing 234–5, *234*
Oriental lamb salad with Thai dressing 235

Pad thai 50
Pan-fried, corn-fed breast of chicken with roasted ceps & Jerusalem artichokes 158, *159*
pancakes
shrimp & green onion pancakes 60, *63*
Rhubarb & elderflower omelette soufflé 18, *19*
Panna cotta al caffé (Coffee-flavoured mascarpone cream) 38, *40*
Panna cotta with spiced oranges *160*, 161
Panzerotti fritti 32
parfaits
Iced vanilla, with roasted nutmeg apples *110*, 111
Pineapple pot-pourri *187*, 188–9
Whisky, with Agen prunes & Earl Grey syrup *148*, 149
Parma ham/prosciutto
Fillet of rabbit roasted in parma ham with fennel confit & chorizo oil *134*, 135
Filo-wrapped asparagus & prosciutto 116
Panzerotti fritti 32
Prosciutto-wrapped chicken breast on cep lentils 68, *69*
Smoked hock & goose liver terrine 181
Vincisgrassi 33
Parsley & garlic sauce 182, *183*
pasta
A minestrone of shellfish *144*, 145
Lasagne of marinated salmon with lemon dressing & chive oil *130*, 131
Panzerotti fritti 32
Vincisgrassi 33
pastry
Filo-wrapped asparagus & prosciutto 116
Raspberry clafoutis in a sweet pastry box with a lemon sabayon 136, *137*
Sweet shortcrust 202
see also dishes made with pastry e.g. tarts
Pavlova roulade with roasted pear *70*, 71
Pea & mint salsa 228, *229*
pea purée, Minted 168, *169*
Peach melba en cage 186, *187*
pears
Pavlova roulade with roasted pear *70*, 71
Pear crisps 249
Roasted, with vanilla ice cream & a chilli froth 249
Pepper oil 142, 168, 246–7, *246*
Pepper "paint" 238–9, *238*
Peppered duck breasts with wild mushroom risotto cakes 198–200, *199*
Pineapple pot-pourri *187*, 188–9
pistachios
Lagan nu custard ("Wedding Custard") 218, *219*
Raspberry & pistachio brûlée with raspberry sorbet *26*, 27
Roast guinea fowl with a pistachio stuffing 170–1
Poached tamarillo with honey yogurt bavarois & brandy snap *230*, 231
polenta, Roast lamb chump on kale & roast garlic polenta with pea & mint salsa 228, *229*
Pommes fondant 170, 240–1, *241*
porcini
Chicken breast stuffed with porcini mushrooms *122*, 123
Vincisgrassi 33
Wild mushroom risotto cakes *199*, 200
pork
Classic wonton soup *92*, 93
Crispy wontons 77
Pork rice paper parcels with sweet & sour coleslaw 244–5, *244*
Thai meatballs 90
Vietnamese-style spring rolls 91
Port-glazed shallots *184*, 185
potatoes
Cod with roasted glazed beetroot & garlic 239
Crocchette d'eglesino affumicato con salsa d'aragosta (Smoked haddock fishcakes with lobster bisque sauce) *34*, 35
Fillet of beef with thyme, red wine & root vegetables *16*, 17
Murghi na pattice (Spiced chicken & potato cakes) 209, *210*
Pan-fried, corn-fed breast of chicken with roasted ceps & Jerusalem artichokes 158, *159*
Pommes fondant 170, 240–1, *241*
Potato salad *22*, 23
Seared calves liver with red cabbage & savoury puy lentils 243
Steamed guinea fowl with mash, artichokes, asparagus & yellow wine sauce 24, *25*
Truffle mash *134*, 135
Warm beetroot & potato salad 246–7, *246*
Potted salmon with potato salad, soured cream & chive oil *22*, 23
Prawns with green curry 80, *81*
prosciutto *see* Parma ham/prosciutto
prunes
Apple, prune & zabaglione tart 124, *125*
Whisky parfait with Agen prunes & Earl Grey syrup *148*, 149
pumpkin custard, Thai-style steamed 87
puy lentils
Cep lentils 68, *69*
Seared calves liver with red cabbage & savoury puy lentils 243

Quail, Quaglie arrosto con salvia e frittedda (Roast, with sage & braised spring vegetables) 36, *37*
quail's eggs, Gourmet delight 179

Rabbit, Fillet of, roasted in parma ham with fennel confit & chorizo oil *134*, 135
ragoût, White bean 181
Raspberry & pistachio brûlée with raspberry sorbet *26*, 27
Raspberry clafoutis in a sweet pastry box with a lemon sabayon 136, *137*
Raspberry coulis 136, *137*
Raspberry sauce *52*, 53, 186, *187*
Raspberry sorbet *26*, 27
Ratatouille 168, *169*
red cabbage & savoury puy lentils, Seared calves liver with 243
Red pepper oil 142, 168, *169*
Red wine sauce *16*, 17, *106*, 107–8, 158
Rhubarb & elderflower omelette soufflé 18, *19*
Rhubarb sorbet 18, *19*
rice
Channa pulao (Chickpea spiced rice) 217
Pork rice paper parcels with sweet & sour coleslaw 244–5, *244*
Spinach & ricotta risotto 120
Sticky 132, *133*
Turmeric 84, *85*
Wild mushroom risotto cakes *199*, 200
Roast fillet of beef with port-glazed shallots *184*, 185
Roast guinea fowl with a pistachio stuffing 170–1
Roast lamb chump on kale & roast garlic polenta with pea & mint salsa 228, *229*
Roast leg of lamb with garlic, rosemary, roasted baby plum tomatoes & broad bean "stew" 146–7
Roast rack of lamb with aubergine caviar 240–1, *241*
Roast sweet potato, coconut & smoked paprika soup with goat's cheese wontons 224, *225*
Roast tournedos of lamb on seared artichoke filled with a cèpe duxelle *106*, 107–8
Roasted baby plum tomatoes & broad bean "stew" 147
Roasted cherry tomatoes *63*, 65
Roasted nutmeg apples *110*, 111
Roasted pear *70*, 71
Roasted pear with vanilla ice cream & a chilli froth 249
root vegetables, Fillet of beef with thyme, red wine & *16*, 17
roulade, Pavlova, with roasted pear *70*, 71

Saffron sauce 182, *183*
Saffron-scented sea bass with warm beetroot & potato salad 246–7, *246*
Saffron water dressing 104, *105*

salads
Chargrilled squid with a spicy coriander salad 236, *237*
Green bean 84, *85*
Oriental lamb, with Thai dressing 235
Potato *22*, 23
Salad of kangaroo fillet with crispy shallots 46, *47*
Seared beef, with spiced beetroot & blue cheese dressing 236–7
Skate & sweet spinach *63*, 64
Vermicelli *156*, 157
Warm beetroot & potato 246–7, *246*
salsa, Avocado 142, *143*, 238–9, *238*
salsa, Pea & mint 228, *229*
sauces *122*, 123
Basil *184*, 185
Béchamel 33
Chilli froth 249
dipping *48*, 49, 77, 91
Ginger 76
Hollandaise 234–5, *234*
Hot & sweet 132, *133*
Lemon sabayon 136
Maraschino sabayon *52*, 54
Parsley & garlic 182, *183*
Raspberry *52*, 53, 186, *187*
Red wine *16*, 17, *106*, 107–8, 158
Saffron 182, *183*
Salsa d'aragosta (Lobster bisque sauce) *34*, 35
Salsa di caffé (Coffee sauce) *40*, 41
Sauce anglaise 18, *19*
Sauce vierge 180
Sweet chilli *226*, 227
Yellow wine 24, *25*
seafood & shellfish
A minestrone of shellfish *144*, 145
Asparagus crown with crab *166*, 167
Chargrilled squid with a spicy coriander salad 236, *237*
Chilli-garlic prawns 60, *63*
Classic wonton soup *92*, 93
Courgette flower filled with seafood 182, *183*
Crispy wontons 77
Grilled scallops with sweet chilli sauce & crème fraîche *226*, 227
Hot & sweet scallops with sticky rice & crab chopsticks 132, *133*
Lobster bisque sauce (Salsa d'aragosta) *34*, 35
Monkfish & mussels in spices 66, *67*
Prawns with green curry 80, *81*
Scallop croûte with sauce vierge 180
Shrimp & green onion pancakes 60, *63*
Singapore curry crab 94, *95*
Tiger prawn chermoula sauté *118*, 119
Ullathiyad (King prawn & scallops with fresh coconut, cumin & vegetables) *214*, 215
Vietnamese-style spring rolls 91
Seared beef salad with spiced beetroot & blue cheese dressing 236–7
Seared calves liver with red cabbage & savoury puy lentils 243
Seared salmon & poached egg with watercress dressing 14, *15*
Seared salmon with Asian coleslaw and a soy-mustard vinaigrette *196*, 197
Seared salmon with rice vermicelli *156*, 157
shallots
Caramelised 104, *105*
Crispy 46, *47*
Port-glazed *184*, 185
Sheek kabab (Minced lamb with spices) 208, *210*
shellfish *see* seafood & shellfish
Sherry dressing 167
Shrimp & green onion pancakes 60, *63*
Singapore curry crab 94, *95*
Skate & sweet spinach salad *63*, 64
Smoked chicken with avocado salsa, herb salad & pepper "paint" 238–9, *238*
Smoked haddock fishcakes with lobster bisque sauce (Crocchette d'eglesino affumicato con salsa d'aragosta) *34*, 35
Smoked hock & goose liver terrine 181
sorbets
Champagne 250–1, *251*
Raspberry *26*, 27
Rhubarb 18, *19*
soufflés
Marinated summer fruits & their soufflé 172
Rhubarb & elderflower omelette soufflé 18, *19*
soups
A minestrone of shellfish *144*, 145
Artichoke & foie gras 14
Classic wonton *92*, 93
Roast sweet potato, coconut & smoked paprika, with goat's cheese wontons 224, *225*
Spiced aubergine, with cumin flatbread 194
Spiced beetroot 236–7
Spiced oranges *160*, 161
Spicy coriander salad 236, *237*
Spicy dipping sauce (Nam prik pla) 77
Spicy stock syrup 189
spinach
Cod with roasted glazed beetroot & garlic 239
Peppered duck breasts with wild mushroom risotto cakes 198–200, *199*
Skate & sweet spinach salad *63*, 64
Spinach & ricotta risotto 120
spring rolls
Crab chopsticks 132, *133*
Vietnamese-style 91
spring vegetables, Braised (Frittedda) 36, *37*
Star anise ice cream *52*, 54
Steamed fish with coconut *78*, 79
Steamed guinea fowl with mash, artichokes, asparagus & yellow wine sauce 24, *25*
Steamed halibut steaks with garlic oil 50, *51*
Sticky rice 132, *133*
stocks 107, 120, 171
sugar cages & spirals *160*, 161, 186, *187*
sugar syrup 186
summer fruits & their soufflé, Marinated 172
Sweet & sour coleslaw 244–5, *244*
Sweet chilli sauce *226*, 227
sweet potato, coconut & smoked paprika soup with goat's cheese wontons, Roast 224, *225*
Sweet shortcrust pastry 202
syrups 149, 186, 189

Tamarillo, Poached, with honey yogurt bavarois & brandy snap *230*, 231
"Tapas-style" starter 60–5, *63*
tartlettes 173, *174*, 175
tarts
Apple, prune & zabaglione 124, *125*
Catalan custard, with a compote of oranges 201–2, *203*
Coconut, with raspberry sauce, star anise ice cream & maraschino sabayon *52*, 53
terrine, Smoked hock & goose liver 181
Thai barbecue chicken *82*, 83
Thai chicken *96*, 97
Thai dressing 235
Thai fishcakes with dipping sauce *48*, 49
Thai meatballs 90
Thai-style halibut with egg noodles 242–3, *242*
Thai-style steamed pumpkin custard 87
Tiger prawn chermoula sauté *118*, 119
tomatoes
Ratatouille 168, *169*
Roasted baby plum tomatoes & broad bean "stew" 147
Roasted cherry *63*, 65
stock 107
Truffle mash *134*, 135
Truffled burrata with roasted cherry tomatoes *63*, 65
tuiles
Chocolate tuile baskets *26*, 27
Tuile baskets 18, *19*, 186, *187*
Tuile biscuits 250–1, *251*
Tuna tartare 179
Tunisian carrot rolls with apricot dip 62, *63*
Turmeric rice 84, *85*

Ullathiyad (King prawn & scallops with fresh coconut, cumin & vegetables) *214*, 215

Vegetables
Fillet of beef with thyme, red wine & root vegetables *16*, 17
Frittedda (Braised spring vegetables) 36, *37*
Ullathiyad (King prawn & scallops with fresh coconut, cumin & vegetables) *214*, 215
Vegetable griddle cakes with soured cream & chives 61, *63*
see also by type e.g. aubergines
Vermicelli salad *156*, 157
Vietnamese-style spring rolls 91
Vincisgrassi 33

Warm beetroot & potato salad 246–7, *246*
Watercress dressing 14
Whisky parfait with Agen prunes & Earl Grey syrup *148*, 149
White bean ragoût 181
Wild mushroom risotto cakes *199*, 200
wonton soup, Classic *92*, 93
wontons, Crispy 77, *196*, 197
wontons, Goat's cheese 224, *225*

Yellow wine sauce 24, *25*
yogurt bavarois, Honey *230*, 231
yogurt dip, Apricot 62, *63*
Yorkshire pudding with foie gras & onion gravy 154, *155*

Zabaglione tart, Apple, prune & 124, *125*

First published in 2000 by HarperCollins*Illustrated*, an imprint of HarperCollins*Publishers*, London

Registered office: Sodexho Limited, Kenley House, Kenley Lane, Kenley, Surrey CR8 5ED.

Editor: Nicola Graimes
Recipe photographs: Frank Wieder
Assistant: Matthew Tugwell
Home Economist: Jane Lawrie
Stylist: Jo Harris
Layout designer: Louise Dick
Indexer: Susan Bosanko

A catalogue record for this book is available from the British Library.

ISBN 0 00 710577 0

Colour origination by Colorscan, Singapore
Printing and bound by Rotolito Lombarda SpA, Italy

Sodexho Limited and the Publishers wish to thank the undermentioned for permission to reproduce the following recipes. Master Class recipe titles may differ from the original recipe titles.

'Panzerotti fritti', 'Panna cotta al caffè', 'Crema bruciata di caffè', 'Gelato al Caffè' and 'Salsa di caffè' from *Franco & Friends: Food from the Walnut Tree* by Franco Taruschio are reproduced with permission of BBC Worldwide Limited. Copyright © Franco Taruschio, 1997.
'Pad Thai' from *At home with Ross Burden* is reproduced with permission of Metro Publishing Ltd. Copyright © Ross Burden 1999.
'"Tapas-style" starter' and 'Prosciutto-wrapped chicken breast on cep lentils' from *The ABC of AWT* by Antony Worrall Thompson are reproduced with permission of Headline Book Publishing Ltd. Copyright © Antony Worrall Thompson 1998.
'Crispy chicken with ginger sauce', 'Crispy wontons', 'Steamed fish with coconut', Prawns with green curry', 'Thai barbecue chicken with green bean salad & turmeric rice', and 'Thai-style steamed pumpkin custard' from *Ken Hom Cooks Thai* by Ken Hom are reproduced with permission of Headline Book Publishing Ltd. Copyright © Ken Hom 1999.
'Thai meatballs', 'Vietnamese-style spring rolls', 'Singapore curry crab', and 'Thai chicken with hong kong-style broccoli and baby corn' from *Ken Hom's Hot Wok* by Ken Hom are reproduced with permission of BBC Worldwide Limited. Copyright © Ken Hom 1996. 'Classic wonton soup' from *Ken Hom's Chinese Cookery* by Ken Hom is reproduced with permission of BBC Worldwide Limited. Copyright © Ken Hom 1987. 'Chocolate cake with candied ginger' from *Travels with a Hot Wok* by Ken Hom is reproduced with permission of BBC Worldwide Limited. Copyright © Ken Hom 1997.
'Ballotine of salmon on caramelised shallots, capers and black olive with a saffron water dressing', 'Roast tournedos of lamb on seared artichoke with a cep cream' and 'Iced vanilla parfait with nutmeg roasted apples' from *New British Classics* by Gary Rhodes are reproduced with permission of BBC Worldwide Limited. Copyright © Gary Rhodes 1999.
'Filo-wrapped asparagus & prosciutto' and 'Tiger prawn chermoula sauté' from *Food of the Sun* by Alastair Little and Richard Whittington are reproduced with permission of Quadrille Publishing Ltd. Copyright © Alastair Little & Richard Whittington 1995. 'Apple, prune & zabaglione tart' reprinted by permission of Conran Octopus Ltd from *Keep it Simple* by Alastair Little © 1993 Alastair Little & Richard Whittington.
'Whisky parfait with agen prunes & earl grey syrup' from *Wild Harvest* by Nick Nairn is reproduced with permission of BBC Worldwide Limited. Copyright © Nick Nairn 1996.
'Panna cotta with spiced oranges' from *The Deli Cookbook* by James Martin is reproduced with permission of Mitchell Beazley. Copyright © James Martin 2000.
'Spiced aubergine soup' and 'Asian coleslaw' from *Ideal Home Cooking* by Paul & Jeanne Rankin are reproduced with permission of IPC Syndication. Copyright © Paul & Jeanne Rankin/Ideal Home/IPC Syndication.
'Kanda bhajia' from Café Spice Namaste by Cyrus Todiwala is reproduced with permission of Ebury Press. Copyright © Cyrus Todiwala 1998.
'Grilled scallops with sweet chilli sauce & crème fraîche' and 'Poached tamarillo with honey yoghurt bavarois & brandy snap' from *The Sugar Club Cookbook* by Peter Gordon are reproduced with permission of Hodder and Stoughton Limited. Copyright © Peter Gordon 1997.

Sodexho Limited have used their best endeavours to ensure permission has been sought for all recipes used where necessary.